Pen & Ink

- Collected Poems -

1968-2008

David Lewis Paget

Barr Books

Dedicated to
my Mother and Father
who each loved literature,
and who instilled in me
a love of
the English language.

All poetry in this book
© 1968-2008
by David Lewis Paget
All Rights Reserved
First Published October 2009

ISBN 978-0-9807148-0-7

Set in 12 point Times New Roman

Published by Barr Books
P.O. Box 172, Moonta 5558
South Australia

Foreword

This is a collection of what I deem to be the more personal poetry written during the first forty years of my writing life. I have decided to place each poem in chronological order, so that my development from simple beginnings may be seen.

Poets are not born, they are made! They begin by possessing both a love of language, and an above average ability in that area; an ability to be able to express themselves. The rest is pure hard work, and an overwhelming desire to hone that gift into a tool which may delight and enthrall others, who, although without the gift, also love fine literature.

The mastery of rhyme and metre should be the goal of every poet. This is a lesson the modernists and post-modernists have forgotten, that for poetry to be assessed as such, it's necessary that it conform to certain disciplines, and those disciplines must be learned. Writing a passage of prose and breaking it down into uneven lines does not constitute a poem. Perhaps these offerings should be called 'Proems', because they are usually thrown off in a fit of the moment, tossed onto the page and forgotten the following day.

For poetry to be memorable it has to be quotable; to be quotable it has to contain certain rhythms and 'hooks' that engage the mind, and make each line easy to recall. It should flow, and contain within it that certain magic which entrances and captures the reader. Hopefully, my later works have accomplished that.

David Lewis Paget

Notes

As this collection is put together in chronological order, there are a few anomalies which should be explained.

1. The 'And...' series of poems were written over several months, so to keep the sequence together it was necessary to ignore the dates that subsequent verses were written, and print them in that sequence.

2. The 'Into the Light' verses were written at ten year intervals, when I was 31, 41, 51 and 61, so they have been grouped together under the date of the first written.

3. I have omitted most of the poems which go to make up the 'Ishtar' series, which were written mainly through 1975-6. These are not intelligible unless read within the context in which they were written. For those who would like to tackle this work in its original form, with all the additional joining pieces added, and explanatory notes, should go to - http://www.angelfire.com/on/ishtar/index.html

4. My three epic poems, 'The Battle of Maldon', 'The Red Knight', and 'Cader Rook' are not represented in these pages, as they comprise a book on their own. For the record, these were composed in 1978, 1980 and 1982.

5. Due to the length of my satire, 'Titan', it has been placed out of sequence at the end of the book.

6. Although there were many other poems written, especially at the beginning of the period in question, the poetry contained in these pages is the only poetry that I consider to be worth saving for posterity - (up until the narrative poetry collections, which are separate from these).

David Lewis Paget

CONTENTS

Index of First Lines 441

-1968-

1. Wessex Bridge 17
2. At Dusk 18
3. Reflections 19
4. Transplant 20

-1969-

5. The Witches 21
6. Spirit 23
7. Wales 25
8. The Poet 26
9. Half Time - No Score 27
10. X-mas 30

-1970-

11. The Tolpuddle Martyrs 31
12. Song of the Jolly Lagger 33
13. The First Fleet - 1787 34
14. The 'Lady Shore' 36
15. The Good Ship Surprize - 1790 37
16. 200 Years After Cook 38
17. The Courtship of John Bryce 38
18. A Tale of Sevenpence Ha'penny 41
19. Divorce Australian Style - 1818 42
20. Dragon Women 43
21. Westgate Bridge Disaster 44
22. Botany Bay 45

-1971-

23. 19 Or'well 48
24. Vision 51

25. Isolat 52
26. That Light - That Sound 53
27. My Love-2 53
28. 1895 Flashlight Society 55
29. Corporal Corporal 58
30. A Letter to My Son 59
31. Peace on Earth 60
32. The Seven Winds 63
33. Borth 65

-1972-

34. Brother Love 67
35. Afterword on the Book of Life 70
36. Stirrup Cup 71
37. Apologia 72
38. Red Sky Warning 74
39. Mary Boots 75
40. The Only Way to Win 76
41. My Generation 39/45 78
42. The Axiom 80
43. Coming Home 80
44. Come Quickly 81
45. Skyjacker 82
46. This is the Way 83
47. Byron Bay 84
48. Death of an Airman 86
49. Scene From A Yamaha 87
50. Pen & Ink 88
51. How Many Men 88

-1973-

52. 1972 89
53. Saturn in the 10th 90
54. Starling 90

55. The Venus Bird 91
56. And 92
57. And...Pt. II 93
58. And...Pt. III 94
59. Castle Walls 96
60. Winterspray 97
61. Half-Remembered 98
62. Nightcaller 100
63. The Deepest Cut 101
64. To Lie in a Caravan 102
65. Mittagong 103
66. Romany Girl 103
67. Dark Forces 104
68. The Old Grey Man of the Sea 105
69. When the Gypsy Crystal Fell 106
70. Love-Lost 107
71. Larkspur 108

-1974-

72. Another Moment More 109
73. Water or Milk 110
74. Three Starlings 110
75. Sweetness and Light 111
76. Cast No Dark Shadows 111
77. Stand Up & Be Counted 112
78. Deadpan 115
79. The Telegram 115
80. The Mother of My Life 116
81. Musicmaker 117
82. Heath - (b. 2 August 1974 d.) 118
83. Lost August 119
84. Jane O'Grady 124
85. Further Down the Line 125
86. Christmas 1974 126

-1975-

87. One Step On 127
88. One Word Swallowed 129
89. Ashes and Dust 129
90. In a Cemetery 130
91. Tallyn Tor 131
92. The Old Wife's Mood 132
93. Déjà vu 133
94. The Wizard of Clayton Close 134
95. Why Do We Write? 136
96. Now That I'm Mad 137
97. The Star 138
98. The Last Trump 139
99. The Morning Sun 140
100. Toll Not My Bell 141
101. Into the Light - (I-V) 142
102. If You Die 145
103. Who Cares? 146

-1976-

104. The Last Word 147
105. The Dog 'Sat' on the Tucker Box 148
106. Losing You 149
107. English Tides 149
108. In Regret 150
109. Short Shrift 151
110. Looking Back (1963-76) 152
111. Scrawled Silence 154
112. Magic Mushrooms 155
113. Horoscope (for Blaise Romany) 157
114. Woman in Child 158
115. 1952 158

-1977-

116. Last Call 159
117. Fireflies 161
118. Clone 162
119. Birmingham 1947 164
120. What Small Dream I? 165
121. The Contract 165
122. For Morgan - (My Son) 166
123. Vignette 167
124. When the Bomb Goes Off 168
125. High 171
126. The Decision 172
127. The Ring Pull Chain 173
128. The Tiger 174
129. Teenage Howl! 176
130. Handsworth Wood 178
131. Father & Son 179
132. Alone 180
133. The Minute Measure 181
134. In the Old Man's House 183
135. A Waking Dream 184

-1978-

136. Before a Custody Case 185
137. The Kelly Curse 186
138. Mortal Cataracts 187
139. One To The Other 188
140. Rad Morgan - (Folk Lyric) 189
141. Grim Seasons 190
142. Post Mortem 191
143. Wych-Elm 192
144. Sir John de Vere 194
145. Stone Cottages 197

146. Static 198
147. For Erika 199
148. Enigma 200
149. Hold As Hold Can 201
150. Lines on a Mormon Missionary 202
151. Burned Out 202
152. Dyes Cast 203

-1979-

153. Palaces of Glass 205
154. One Lonely Night 206
155. The Fairy Light 207
156. The Fourth Horseman 208
157. After the Bomb 210
158. Yellowcake 211
159. At Eaglehawk Neck 212
160. Sea and Shore 213
161. In Retrospect 215
162. Words 216
163. Stars 216
164. Home acre 217
165. Tack & Edge 218
166. Late of Days 219

-1980-

167. Poverty Grass 220
168. For Leslie - (a 21 year old divorcee) 221
169. Milady Gay 222
170. Port Hughes Re-visited 223
171. For a Dreamer 223
172. Before the Storm 224
173. Brick by Brick 225
174. Threads 225
175. Grasmere 226

176. My Daughters Dear 228
177. Bad Blood 229
178. Against the Rain 230
179. Surge 231
180. On the Passing of my 36th Year 231
181. On the Death of John Lennon 232
182. Contage - (a conversational montage) 233

-1981-

183. A Welsh Hymn 234
184. Vain Imaginings 236
185. Party Trick 237
186. Pas de Deux 238
187. A Canticle for Wakeman 239
188. The Sentinel 241
189. To an Artist 242
190. Time Knows No Passages 243
191. Careless Lines 243
192. Five Children I 244
193. Sonnet - on My 37th Year 245

-1982-

194. 1981 246
195. Where Cobwebs Line 247
196. Danse de la Morte 248
197. The Pen 250
198. You & I 251
199. Before the British Fleet 252
200. The Basic Tenets 253
201. 2May82 - The Falklands 254
202. All Things Burn Slowly 254
203. Tennos pour Lorac 255
204. On the Execution of a Mural 256
205. On the Raising of the Mary Rose 258

206. Beyond the Breach 259
207. Blake 262

-1983-

208. Old Shades 263
209. By Miners Hands 264
210. Chimneys of Lime 265
211. An Old Coast 266
212. To Keep My Wanton 268
213. From Line to Grid 269
214. Tinder Box 270
215. Dinosaurs 271
216. From a Blue Cloud 272
217. Moon-Wake 273
218. Spill Your Tears 274
219. On Receiving Your Letter for My 39th Grief 276

-1984-

220. Audition 278
221. Pengellen 279
222. For a Social Worker 281
223. Catherine Gables 282
224. Twenty Years Down - (The Beatles) 284
225. Spoils of War 285
226. Mother of Sons 286
227. Does She Stalk Pathways 287
228. Spend and Grieve 289

-1985-

229 Tongues of Torns 290
230. Before We Part 291
231. Waters Into Wine 292
232. I Work Machines 293
233. The Abbey 294

234. Love Grows Slowly 295
235. On My 2 Year Old, Leaving 296
236. It! 297
237. Do What You Will! 298
238. Bitter Heart! 299
239. One September Night 300
240. Once, When the World of Trees 301

-1986-
241. On Leaving C.Y.S.S. 302
242. Beached Morning 303
243. Questing 304
244. Well We Might 306

-1987-
245. Old Pain 307
246. Angel Head 308
247. On the Death of My Father 308
248. Aftermath 309
249. The Bloodletting 311
250. Sink or Swim 312

-1988-
251. Theme for a New Daughter 313
252. Sonnet on Loss 314

-1989-
253. Sanctuary 314
254. Stalemate 316
255. Ship to Shore 317

-1990-
256. Where Once the Dreaming 319

-1991-

257. Trench Warfare 320
258. Outlived 321
259. Never the God 322
260. When Our Days Are Minutes 323

-1992-

261. Dissolution 324
262. For Lyn 325
263. Condemned to Partings 325
264. Tablets of Jet 326

-1993-

265. In Ancient Time 327
266. On My Mother's 80th 329

-1994-

267. When the Welsh of Wales Go Home 330
268. In Your Dark, Slated Halls 331
269. White Horses 332
270. Maps & Charts 333

-1996-

271. The Turncoat 335

-1997-

272. How the Eye Deceives 339

-1998-

273. Passenger from Childhood 340
274. Early Morning Call 341
275. On Your 48th 342

-1999-

276. The Book of Numbers 343
277. Nostradamus 344
278. The Water Tower 345
279. No-Name the Cat 347

-2005-

280. One by One 348
281. Into the Light - III (repeated) 349
282. China 350
283. Where are the Birds of Wenzhou, Bei Bei 350
284. Black-Haired Girls 352
285. The Man in the Chinese Moon 353
286. Blue Mountain Coffee 354
287. Dragons 356

-2006-

288. Terra Cotta Warrior 359
289. Riding the Wenzhou Bus 360
290. Swan Song 362
291. Bibles 365
292. I Can't Find a Doll with a Chinese Face! 366
293. The Blueshell Bar 367
294. Pu Tong Hua 369
295. Tense, You Buggers, Tense! 370
296. Beautiful Flower 371
297. Don't Let Me Die in China, Lord! 372
298. The Crazy Lady of Jiao Ba Lu 375
299. Chingl-ai 378
300. The Endless Taxi 379
301. Before I Forget 382
302. The Beggar of Wu Ma Jie 384

-2007-

303. I Waste My Days 385
304. A Pensioners Prayer 386
305. Why Does My Faith 387
306. Goddo & Me 389
307. To My Wives 391
308. Dong Tou Dao 392
309. Somebody, Help! 393
310. China Song – (Zhōng guó gē qǔ) 394
311. The Burglar Dog 395

-2008-

312. Shoes 397
313. Obit 399
314. Would He Even Know Me Now? 400
315. Getting Old 401
316. While I Write and Breathe 402
317. I Must Have Been Sleeping 404
318. Winter Comes 406
319. Woman 407
320. Skipping! 409
321. What's in a Name? 410
322. www. 411
323. Isabel Allende 413
324. What Happened to the Day? 414
325. The Attic 416
326. The Melbourne Cup 418

A Parody - (1982)

327. Titan 419
328. Notes on 'Titan' 433

-1968-

Wessex Bridge

It would not snow at Wessex Bridge
So there I had to go,
To take away degrees of heat
And freeze the sentry, on his beat,
To chill the earth through many feet
But still it would not snow!

I saw the wind at Wessex Bridge
That rushed in from the north,
Its icy blast had worked in lace
Its horror on a soldier's face
And left him in a bitter case,
But still it would not snow!

A cloud hung over Wessex Bridge
A cloud that would not rain,
You do your best and leave the rest
We'll freeze the drops in mocking jest
And spread in white an ample vest,
Our words were all in vain.

There's carnage here at Wessex Bridge
A battle lost and won,
Where blood is frozen in a stream,
The slaughtered lie as in a dream
Of horror in an awful scene
Of death that has been done.

It would not snow at Wessex Bridge
And now I think I know,
Just why the dead are left to lie
To jar the sense, assault the eye,
For nature will not be allied
To cover up man's grisly show.

May 1968

At Dusk

I stand alone on Wentworth Hill
And own the green grass of the world,
I see the last, old weathered trees
And breathe the end of sweet, pure air.
Then I just sit and take it in,
This all, this last of everything
Before it's gone, and Wentworth Hill
Becomes another thoroughfare.

But now I feel this Wentworth Hill
Belongs to me, for I am man,
And all this was bequeathed to me
So for it, I should take a stand.
But who am I, the fettered soul
Of man's desire for beauty, and
Subordinate to his machines
That tear apart this aching land.

And as I sit on Wentworth Hill
I'm looking down on man's attempt

To build his paradise in stone;
To brush aside in low contempt
The paradise that nature laid,
His smoke and soot and grey cement
And ferroconcrete structures rise
To brush the skies in wonderment.

The end is near for Wentworth Hill,
The last hill man may ever mock
As metal monsters tear its heart
To conquer nature with their shock.
To girdle concrete round the earth
And leave no nature seal unlocked,
And as all beauty dies with it
The world is left… a window box.

June 1968

Reflections

A raindrop from the womb am I,
A snowflake drifting through the sky
Or cobweb floating lightly down
And ever closer to the ground.

And those who went before, I see
As dampness, spreading carelessly,
Upon the spot where now they lie
As in the end, we all must die.

So that is all there is to life?
A birth of condensated sound,

A certain flight through wind and light
To certain death, upon the ground.

But what lies further, and beyond;
Is that the end there, on the ground,
Or does the damp evaporate
And rise again, to condensate?

November 1968

Transplant

Still and grey in death he lies
So grey his face, so grey his eyes,
And in his flesh the windscreen glass
Which cut his face, and helped him pass;
But in his chest a hole to fill,
The heart that beat is beating still.

It beats within an older man
Reprieves those older, trembling hands,
It's such a pity that he'll die,
For die he will, the odds are high,
But Doctors still maintain the right
To fight the good Creator's might.

A mother weeps out in the hall
The pure despair that death gives all,
And in her agony of mind
The answer now she tries to find,
It's just a question, softly said:
'That grey young man now - was he dead?'

December 1968

-1969-

The Witches

How much further to Warwick?

Seventy four on floating wheels
And carrying thirteen pretty girls
Who chant and smile, and pat their curls
And set their sights on Warwick.

How much further to Warwick?

Sixty-six and that's a fact
With thirteen mouths to chant the act
For thirteen girls no going back
They have to get to Warwick.

How much further to Warwick?

Fifty-five so set your brooms
And laugh your magic in the gloom
To weave your spell of certain doom
On all the men in Warwick.

How much further to Warwick?

Forty-four to wend your way
The day is dark, the night is grey
The witches Sabbath month of May
Is covening in Warwick.

How much further to Warwick?

Thirty-three so spend your time
In sipping heady summer wine,
And mixing potions, bending minds
In preparation for Warwick.

How much further to Warwick?

Twenty-two and spiders legs
With serpents' blood and turtle eggs
Are boiling in the cauldron dregs
Of thirteen witches of Warwick.

How much further to Warwick?

Thirteen miles and thirteen brooms
Of thirteen witches in the gloom
Are flying now beneath the moon
And homing in on Warwick.

How much further to Warwick?

Only three that I can see
The witches cackle now with glee
The devil's only pedigree
Will now convene in Warwick.

How much further to Warwick?

Nothing now, and looking fresh
Are thirteen girls in fancy dress,
Nothing more - and nothing less,
The hit of the ball at Warwick!

6 January 1969

Spirit

'I died early,' said the Spirit,
'So I didn't have the chance to learn,
And though I don't exactly burn
With envy for your thirty years,
It's such a pity dying young,
The pleasures of a youth, unsung…
For all I left behind of me
Were memories of my mother's pain
In birth and death,
Though such a breath of time it took,
It's hard to judge that I had been,
That any could remain.
But for my father's constant hurt,
His burden through a lonely life
Was such to crush the living breath
Right out of him, but could I see,
And crush the death right out of me.'

'I hunger then, for knowledge
Of the seven wonders of the world
And nature's secrets, all unfurled
As life unfolds before a man;
Of seas and skies and mountains high,
The visions of an inner eye,
And colours I have ever longed for,
Colours I have never seen,
Though I have dreamed,
(Poor substitute it is for truth);
I need the miracle of sight,
The senses in-between,
Which add your touch and taste and smell

To that of thought, which now I am,
A lonely thought communicating in itself
Its loneliness,
Your knowledge is an untold wealth.'

'I envy you,' I then replied,
'For ignorance of man's affairs
Is rarely found,
And one who cares is better off
To never know.
But since you must insist to hear
The seven wonders are but fear
Of War, that selfish slaughter leaving
Millions dead and millions maimed,
And poverty, when countless numbers
Starve to death,
Diseases raging through a stricken land
To our undying shame
And apathy to suffering,
The depths of immorality,
And crime and violence in the streets
That holds a sway on everyone,
Commercial greed is God today.'

The Spirit sighed a troubled sigh;
'An answer such as this unwanted
Tale of human misery and suffering
I'd not prepared for,
Makes me care for man no less, but
Takes me back and leaves me low.
A thousand years of meditation
On these things may mend my wound,
But now I cry, and go to find

A quiet place…
My innocence will not repair,
Not now or even soon!'

And so he sadly turned away,
In seconds then was lost to view,
I shouted that I meant to say
We still have hope…
But he was gone.

If we have time, I'll never know!

January 1969

Wales

Find me a coast where the sea rolls in
And the shingles reach down to the shore,
Where the sand is as soft as a woman's skin
And the cliffs are the ultimate law,
Where the rock pools are hid when the tide is up
And the sky is as grey as a stone,
Where the man of the land has a plentiful cup
And there I shall make my home.

Find me a land where the people speak
In a strange and a colourful tongue,
Find me a land where the seagull's beak
Looks out, to comfort its young.
Find me a land where the men can sing
So fine, it tears the eye;
Find me the land I'm yearning
For there my bones will lie.

Find me a cottage, thatched with straw
And find me a blue-eyed maid,
My life shall I wander by the shore
With my wife in her pretty braid;
To watch white horses galloping in
Through all the winter gales,
Find me a land where the sea rolls in,
Find me a land called Wales…

13 February 1969

The Poet

The poet lives up on a windy hill
In a cottage of whitewashed stone,
A thatch that will leak in a winter's gale
But a place he can call his home.
As he sits on the worn, old white-washed step
For a smoke of his gnarled old pipe,
He seeps in the feeling of utter content
To carelessly paint in the words of his time,
The things that he sees, for they're always in rhyme,
And everything's heaven sent!

The poet lives up on a jagged cliff
A background of seagulls and blue,
The monument near to the ship that was wrecked
He paints in a vivid hue,
And sailors spring out of a sprawling page
To cry out their faint surprise,
The sky turns to grey on a thunderous day,
The sailors must swim when the lightning strikes,
Braving the storm to head in for the lights…
Now what will the poet say?

The poet lives up on a grassy knoll,
The village is further below,
And children are warned not to speak to him
For fear of losing their souls.
His poetry still will attract them all
As the characters come to life;
For the smugglers light may be seen in the night,
The pirates will bury their ill-gotten gold,
Whenever the weather is chilly and cold
The poet is said to write.

The poet lives up on a windy hill
In a cottage of whitewashed stone,
A thatch that will leak in a winter's gale
But a place he can call his home.
He conjures up visions of military men
And hears them go 'tramp' in the night,
While the villagers shutter their window-sills,
He wistfully waits for the sound of the lark,
And then, late at night, he just turns on the dark,
The poet is sitting there still.

March 1969

Half Time - No Score!

A scanner in Greenland relaying the score,
The man in the grey flannel suit is directing
The traffic, and checking
His manual on quaint International Law,
The section that covers correction of lovers
And touches on quaint International War.

In London and Moscow the people are waiting,
In Peking and Washington, calculating
The minutes of meetings and protest marches
The cost of concealing those sabotages
Of missiles now speeding toward the umbrellas
As someone is running a four minute mile,
To check at his own private atom bomb shelter
In hopes that the referees whistles and rules
Are succeeding in keeping them off for a while.

A bottle of Burgundy must be enjoyed at half time
So the light turns to red with no score,
But China is playing the game with the rules
Of Mah Jongg, and collecting the dragons and flowers,
As short April showers are falling in Liverpool,
Sydney is bounced off the satellite, two-up school
Going on calmly in Melbourne as usual,
Transistors blaring Australian Rules.
But the Rest of the world can't be bothered to listen
The scoreboard is showing to Russia one-nil...
Though the Great Britain team has surprised
With a sneaky disguise in the guise of a
Virus from Rhyl.

The only American Man in the Moon
Is too high on hallucinogen to be useful
For ought but to classify Moon-branded cheese;
The Vietnam delegate gets off his knees
In a mushroom he helped manufacture in Hanoi
And wonders if Paris was not a mistake,
To be too dogmatic, a Russian romantic
Is raptured to bring down Imperial Power
For the revolution of shooting recruiting
May be the solution to western aggression

While Arsenal beat the United once more
And a famous explorer climbs up to the top
Of the North-West Pole for the umpteenth time,
A pacifist asks if they ever will stop,
This conscription is giving a very hard time
On a Sunday, always he wishes for Monday,
Glued to his pew with a sickly smile,
He's reading the first second chapter of John,
And punctuates nicely the sound of the bombs.

At: the Tab they're all waiting the final result,
The old Australian betting cult
Could not resist giving Russia the odds
In the war with China,
But Waltzing Matilda with President Somebody-Else,
They're saying, that Britain could want
Nothing finer than peace
And a place in the Market,
As London subsides to sink
Solemnly into the wandering Thames.
While tanks from Detroit keep on rolling on rolling
In time to the rhythm of lend-lease for Israel
Playing the Arabs at middle-east games.
Russia is one and America three, calling England...
Just radio genuine claims, reading
Two for Great: Britain and one more for China
That turned in the air to demolish Peking,
So just give me the half time no score somebody,
Can you not hear that I'm speaking...
Can you not hear that I'm speaking...
Can you not hear?

April 1969

X-Mas

The season is heralded first by the trees,
Sprouting in windows
    And waving in breezes of coloured lights,
That spark the delight in the eyes of the children
    Of Jesus Christ.

The shops full of tinsel and holly and crepe,
Mark up the prices,
    A man who is draped in a tunic and beard,
His hand grasping out as they sit on his knee for
    The Christmas cheer.

Bumper to bumper, the cars on their way
To paradise places,
    The posters to say not to drink when you drive,
The bodies they scrape off the highways and byways
    That didn't arrive.

Blood on the tunic and red on the road,
Children and giving,
    Our gifts are the load of the three wise kings,
Our slaughter is part of the sort of men's folly
    That Cross-mas brings.

December 1969

-1970-

The Tolpuddle Martyrs

'I break my back on many a rock,
And tramp for many a mile,
With an iron clamp on my weary leg
And a chain that frets for a while,
A road to build in the searing heat,
An iron gang shuffling on,
We swing the pick, we clear the track
And curse the road that we've done.'

'The road is a trail of blood, my friend,
The road is a trail of pain,
The work is slow and laborious
For we have nothing to gain,
But the sting of the lash of 'justice'
The magistrate's able friend,
And the hope of a ticket-of-leave, so we
May hold up our heads again.'

'A labouring man I used to be
A labouring man I am,
Though Tolpuddle is a far acry
From Melbourne's hellish land,
For he sent us out on a passing whim,
He turned his back on our cry,
And he tells the Queen it must surely be
As he hopes we'll silently die.'

'But I'll not go off through swinging a pick
For this is my very life,

Though the sweat and toil may wear me down
And I'll cry at the thought of my wife,
But then if the brute should spring to life
I'll struggle to hold it down,
To preserve the light of my sanity
In this hell-hole, Sydney Town.'

'A Union we had thought to begin
By swearing allegiance to it,
Uniting the plight of the working class
And willing to suffer to do it,
But Melbourne martyred the foundling scheme
And started a flame so bright,
Within all the hearts, within all the minds
Of the followers of the right.'

'So one-two-three, I swing the pick
And give out a savage cry,
One-two-three, Lord Melbourne's son
Will see the fruit of his father's try
To shackle the working class in chain,
And keep them the slaves of the land,
As Tolpuddles everywhere will rise
With their working class demands.'

January 1970

Song of the Jolly Lagger

'We come from Shoreditch
               Gorbals
                             Bishopsgate
Clerkenwell, Spitalfields and old St. Giles,
The ladies on the town and the gents on the dip,
And the capital coves from the old hulk ship.
I've been on the cross since eleven or so
And I've pushed a few down for a bob,
But the nosers get a little too hot for a lag
And the runners do a bad-cess job.'

'I've been to Brixton
               Newgate
                             Maidstone
Bridewell, Compter, and once in Steel,
Manning was hanging and his wife turned off
As I found a new watch on a Park Lane toff.
I met me a man with a tattooed arm
And a prostitute known as Nell,
We were nailed by the sale of the lead from a church
With a journey that we couldn't quite sell.'

'I've gone through Jackson
                   Norfolk
                               Maquarie
Ports Arthur and Phillip, Van Diemen's curse,
I've dragged a lot of chain, and I've done a lot of time
And I took a lot of lash on this back of mine;
But I never did sing when the cat came down
Though I took to the bush when I could,

The bushranging life for a shiftless man
Does his soul quite a power of good.'

'We come from Shoreditch
            Gorbals
                  Bishopsgate
Clerkenwell, Spitalfields and old St. Giles,
Living in the shadows of the well-worn gallows
Of the cat-o-nine tails and the capital coves.
See 'em turned off as we dipped for a guinea
Or pitched and tossed for a shilling,
If I had it all again I'd still be a lag…
While money's still money, and my pockets keep filling.'

January 1970

The First Fleet – 1787

'The creaking hulks of rotten, rat-infested vermin in the Thames
Must be removed,' the cry was heard;
'The prison ships of groaning filth are rattling their chains!'
Gin soaked hags and dismal lags,
Felons in their petty way,
And Irish rebels on their knees will feel Brittania's mighty sway.

'The product of a nation's waste, from gutter, inn and grimy port
Must not be seen,' the righteous cry.
'The slatterns from the tavern door must certainly be taught!'
Highwaymen and Jack the Dip
Are waiting for the gibbet cart,
While children thieves to sell as slaves can but await their barter.

Groaning underneath the weight of misery and malcontent
The First Fleet sailed, in eighty seven,
Spitting out from Spithead all the spite that British law could vent;
Bearing it a world away,
Shackled in the stinking hold
With curses falling on the air they left dear England's wanton fold.

The 'Sirius' was Phillip's ship, a hundred feet in length throughout,
On this marines were safely decked;
But 'Friendship', 'Charlotte', 'Prince of Wales', and 'Scarborough'
                                                                                         no doubt,
'Alexander', 'Lady Penrhyn'
Echoed to those cries of pain that
Even now ring down the ages, screaming England's mortal shame.

Cruelly tormented people, shuttered in and cast away
Who had to bide such bitter time
To found that 'colony of thieves' in distant New South Wales;
From your convict loins have sprung
The new-found nation's hardy sons
Who look with pride, and stand beside the very first Australians.

January 1970

The 'Lady Shore'

What's in a name, 'Lady Shore',
Who was to blame for the shame you saw,
Billowing sail, carry the tale
Of the 'Lady Shore' with its women aboard,
Seized by the military guard.

What's in a sigh, glistening eye,
Convicts in dresses with long, long tresses,
Feminine wiles, dressed in the styles
Of the Flash houses, falling apart at the seams,
Burying long-lost dreams.

What's in a place, loss of grace,
Coarsening charm on a tattooed arm,
Final despair, nobody cares
If you've been on the town and you're still going down,
Your life for the theft of a pound.

What's in a trip, sailing ship,
Sydney, or anywhere no-one can stare,
Living and love, light from above
That will keep you away from those factory pains,
Free of Port Jackson chains.

What's in a lie, freedom or die,
Sailing you sixty and six women by,
Turbulent swell, bidding you well;
But what has befallen the lost 'Lady Shore',
Not to be heard of more?

30 January 1970

The Good Ship 'Surprize' – 1790

Surprize!……………………..Surprize!

Hell ship sailing in to shore
Its groaning timbers groaning more
As Reverend Johnson went to see
The convicts great indignity.
Naked men of lice and chain,
Such hopelessness within their eyes
Could well begin the sad refrain:

Surprize!…………………….Surprize!

Bodies cast upon the rocks
As tortured voices cried: 'A pox
On British justice and its way.'
The feeble fade and dying lay,
Creeping on all fours ashore
The breath of life within them cries
And Satan chants in growing roar:

Surprize!…………………….Surprise!

Johnson gazed across the sea:
'Is this what horror means to me?'
And eighty six all buried deep,
A troubled death, a troubled sleep.
Sent his call to Wilburforce
To try and right the spurious lies
So dead no more will ever call:

Surprize!…………………….Surprize!

March 1970

200 Years After Cook

Would Cook, I wonder, ever have dreamt
Of seventeen eighty-eight,
Of convict ships and dismal cargoes
Rushing onward to their fate?
As he sailed the eastern waters
Did he see the prison yards,
Were the gallows, gaunt and tall
Surrounded by the spectral guards?
Did he hear the groans and cries,
The cat 'o nine, its evil hiss…
Could he possibly have known
Discovery would come to this?

April 1970

The Courtship of John Bryce

John Bryce set sail on a winter's morn,
A hell-ship, travelling south,
His spirit so low as to match the
Noisome ashes in his mouth,
And he felt the craft of the Smithy's trade,
A chastening, sad reminder,
And he felt the wind as it caught the sail
Following on behind her.

Bryce was a man who had kicked a Lord
On a drunken spending spree,
'Bryce', said the judge, 'you'll assuredly hang
For this piece of villainy.'
But they sent him on to the prison hulks,

They tossed a coin on his fate,
And he found himself in the foetid air
Of the 'Neptune's' sorry state!

At once assigned to a freeman's land
In the colony's lawful way,
With seven long years of purgatory
To hold him in their sway,
He kept his peace and he bent his back
To the task, so not to grieve,
And before too long he had earned respect
And a welcome ticket-of-leave.

But he stayed and he worked for wages then,
For wages and for rum,
And he spent his nights at the tavern door,
(Would his freedom never come?)
For the loneliness was eating away
At his convict's sorry life,
Would it help at all if he settled him down
And took a factory wife?

So come on down to the factory
And look the ladies over,
You'll have a choice of the best
This foundling colony can offer.
Set your sights on their buxom charms
The prettiest you can find,
But beware that the tongue of the viper
Is the one you leave behind.

John Bryce paid heed to the wisdom of
His master's sound advice,
And along the line of a hundred strong
He tried to make his choice,

When a wench with a bold, resentful air
He suddenly espied,
Her hair in a coil that would look so fair
When he made the girl his bride.

He gave her the sign to step aside
Which she did, as bold as brass,
A sway of the hips to show how
Wonderfully well she filled her dress.
'What makes you think that you're good enough?'
The Irish colleen said;
'I have to judge if you are that,'
Young John replied instead.

'Now when I take this bride of mine
She must be ever true,
None of this old flirtatious stuff
You Irish colleens do,
And in my house my word will be
Regarded as the law,
So think you quickly on it
And we'll dally here no more.'

'I like the cut o' your jib, me bhoy,
Though nothing to goggle at.'
He said: 'You're right, and yerself is fairly plain
To come to that.'
'Well that's a fine upstanding thing
To say to a future bride!'
'Oh, there's more, but I'll let it rest
'Til I can beat your pretty hide.'

'So, beating is it? Lord, that you should
Ever have the nerve,

I'll black your eye in a trice if you
Should look at a pretty curve.'
'Well then, we seem agreed on just
Exactly what we're at,
The curves you have will amply
Suit my appetite for that.'

No more did poor John Bryce stand lonely
Out by the tavern door,
No more did Sheila have to stand
And weave on the factory floor.
Their children three would all agree
She never looked askance,
And John himself was always true
To her Irish countenance.

28 April 1970

A Tale of Sevenpence Ha'penny

(Based on the experience of an early governor of the new penal settlement at Moreton Bay, Queensland).

'I would like, good sirs,
To make it known,
Whether you heed or not,
That the Treasury here at Moreton Bay
Scarcely helped a lot!
A miserable sevenpence ha'penny
Hardly seems enough,
A question here would seem sincere;
How to divide it up?'

'A penny for roads to suit our needs,
A tuppenny bridge or two?
Three ha'pence worth of food should amply
Satisfy the convict crew.
A penny to spend on Government House
Is all I really dare,
And tuppence I'll leave in the Treasury
To supply us with coal for the year.'

'I would like, good sirs,
To make it known,
Whether you heed or not,
That a thief has entered the Treasury
And taken the blooming lot!
The fault is mine, I must admit
I should have thought to guard it,
But such a sum had gone to my head
And left me quite retarded.'

May 1970

Divorce Australian Style – 1818

'My wife has walked away with herself again,
Took to a man on a cattle run, poor fellow,
Left a note to say she'd gone
And thought to share another bed,
She'd better not come back running to me, tomorrow.'

'Now I'll make it plain and public said to all,
For bite and sup I will not pay at all… for Honey!

And if she contracts on my name,
(Now don't be caught, she has the hide),
Then you'd better go off and find her again, for money.'

'I'm not a man to carry a grudge for long,
Never a man to raise a fuss for nowt... by golly,
But she cost me a blue-ribbon pig, you know,
A pig and a bushel of wheat, my lad,
And a gallon of rum that *I* never got to swallow!'

May 1970

Dragon Women

Merlin-magic, mixing potions
Misty towers, ghostly sway,
Take the sword from out the granite,
Table round a roundelay.

Dragons breath in blazing flashes,
Armoured knights to join the fray,
Lances glitter in the sunlight,
Maiden, castle-locked away.

Float a ballroom round in satin
Garter dropped, a lady's shame,
Look around to quell the glances,
Chivalry of later fame.

Hansom cabs and flowing dresses,
Women play a ladies game,
Statuesque, with hidden beauty,
Timelessness within a frame.

Suffragettes and iron railings
Chained to vote beside a fence,
Leap before a Derby runner,
Count the cost, but not expense.

Motors belching carbon vapours,
Women streaming in to earn,
Nylon ladders rushing onward,
Tramline strap, a chafing burn.

Take a seat and hurry forward,
Equal pay and unisex,
Dragon street-fed children in
And don't forget the suffragettes!

July 1970

Westgate Bridge Disaster - 1970

A crane stands gaunt against the sky
Its towering form impersonal,
                        incapable of thought,
But could a crane but see and feel
The air would fill with tears of steel
Or else be set at naught.

The day the Westgate bridge came down
A grinding roar to terrify,
                        intensify the shock,
A stunned announcer shook his head
A city waited for the dead
Then started taking stock.

The workers on the bridge were hard,
Harder men and tougher men,
      tougher men you'll rarely find.
But tears were shed for mates' distress
By men that cry for nothing less,
There's nothing less to mind.

What gives a moment prominence?
The crash of steel, the rivets stripping
      ripping like machine-gun fire,
Plunging concrete, flying mud
The screams of dying, dirt and blood,
Or men that never tire?

Rescuers, appalled and heartsick
Plunging tireless, never ending,
      sending hope within the span!
Some will never see November
Westgate bridge we'll all remember,
Tribute to the warmth of man.

October 1970

Botany Bay

In April 1770, 'Endeavour' put to sea,
And left behind New Zealand shores
To set fair weather westward course
For in command Lieutenant Cook
Had hopes of great discovery;
(A southern continent as large as Europe lay in wait);
So Cook sailed on, as dolphins made

Their leaping, wandering friendship known,
The albatross soared overhead,
And Joseph Banks looked out his gun
To take the lumbering giant home!

The sixteenth day a sparrow came
To rest upon the deck.
A gannet held a westward course,
The weather broke, a sudden squall
Cut out the light from straining sight
As on they ploughed through restless seas
Until Lieutenant Hicks cried out upon the nineteenth day:
'Land lies ahead, thank God,' he said,
And stood towards the distant shore
'Til fifteen miles from land so green
They turned aside, and ran along
This virgin country… Nevermore!

The wind and rain kept up their bitter,
Miserable attack,
And waterspouts were seen to rise
To merge with grey and dismal skies,
But soon it cleared, the land endeared
To all by fertile, sloping hills,
And through the trees a wisp of smoke
Was curling softly up.
Then in the glass, dark men were seen,
The owners of this green expanse,
But still 'Endeavour' headed north
To pass the white of chalky cliffs
That nature set down to entrance.

In April, on the 28th, an opening in the cliffs,
'Endeavour' headed in for shore

And Cook in his excitement saw
The natives pulling fish in from
Their strange canoes of weathered bark
And huts set down at random, as if
Set there by a painter's art.
But when they tried to row ashore
The natives menaced with their spears,
And though the odds were all against
It took a shot from Cook to set them
Running for their wooden shields.

Stingrays in the Bay, to Cook,
Bethought him most appropriate,
But Banks was charmed with plants and trees
And things pertained to botany.
The ghostly gums and gnarled young saplings
Braced against the gentle breeze
Kept Parkinson, the artist, sketching likeness as they stood.
So Cook said: 'Feast your English eyes
And hoist the Union Jack, you see,
Upon our great New Holland prize!
For this,' cried Cook, 'must surely be
A wondrous Bay of Botany.'

December 1970

-1971-

19 Or'well

I'm shivering in the afterglow
Surrounded by the early snow
That laps at Melbourne's frozen feet,
And sheltering from the withering blast
Of hail and sleet, in late November,
Trying to remember what
The sun was like before the war,
That no-one felt, that no-one saw
That wiped a memory out before
The rocket sputtered off to Mars
And left us wondering what to do
About the rats, that roam the streets,
Infest the yards,
And make their nests in motor cars...

Motor cars that rust in line,
Incredible things from another time
That must be future, can't be past;
The pain of knowing what we lost
Is just too much assimilation...
Let it be enough to say
That Sydney Harbour glows at night,
A soft green, all-pervading light,
And if the Harbour Bridge was ever
Anything beside a dream
A sudden flash awoke a scream
In driver's throats, in different notes,

That had no time to issue forth
Before the Bridge they travelled on,
Their motor cars, and they, were gone;

So if a million photographs
Have faded out to nothingness,
A million family trees of note
Have fallen to the ground,
It only goes to show the imbecilic
Fickleness of man, so tell me
How do I begin to shut the factory down?

I'm staggering up an icy street
Trying to disregard the feet
That nature didn't give me black,
And searching for a hidden store,
The food I lack has all been looted.
Men are shooting, men are shooting men
Are running round in packs,
In self defence, for nothing lacks
A moral if you search for one;
I've even seen a woman eat
Her baby's flesh, out in the road
In Collins Street,
And gag on it, and choke it out,
And wash it down with Cooper's stout.

Why was Melbourne left to die
Uncivilised and haltingly in
Soul destroying self-destruction....
If the bomb's eruption had not
Decimated Dandenong, but travelled on
And blasted Bourke's black heart along the

Soul of Swanston's timeless beat,
At least the end would be much neater....

Sitting round and waiting for the end are many
Troubled men, in every bar
That has a stock,
And brandy flows, and whisky goes
The product of a countryside that
Lies beneath a boiling sea,
A Scotland, name that used to be...

But in the gutter lies a man who
Died just half an hour before
His mate could find a dying priest
To say a muttered prayer:
"You always were a tricky swine
You pommie bastard," said the man
And shed a tear of self reproach
Before he turned
To leave him there.

10 February 1971

Vision

I'm waiting for a number nine
To take me on to Jindabyne
Though why I want to go I can't recall,
And as the traffic passes by
It's just as if a rubber sigh
Is oozing up to tell us of our fall.
    And all the eyes are sightless, look ahead,
      For all the minds behind the eyes are dead!

I'm drifting in a crystal sea
A wandering nonentity
And crying out in hopes that I'll be heard,
But sinking under waves of thought
And knowing all will come to nought
I'll never have the strength to pass the word;
    And all the old ideas carry on,
      With all the brains behind them dead and gone!

I'm heaving at the length of chain
That's clamped and shackled to my brain
Rejecting everything I've ever learnt,
And watching for the man in time
Whose slogan banners bend the mind
And hoping that the people see them burnt.
    But all I see is misery to come,
      Regrets will pave the path that we've begun.

I'm waiting for a number nine
To take me on to Jindabyne
Though why I want to go I can't recall,
But I can see the tidal wave

That's rushing on through this decade
And backing every man against the wall;
   We'll have to turn and face it now, or run,
   I'll pause along the way and buy a gun!

17 March 1971

Isolat

His eyes are sharp, and glitter
From a face of city litter, looking out
From parking lots, and a thousand city blocks,
And the traffic that surrounds him, and the pavement
And the street, and the prisons and the missions and
The drag of many feet!

His skin is old and weathered
And his face is tough as leather, drifting on
Through giant stores, and a thousand crystal doors,
And the high-rise slums that claim him, and the cheaper
Type of wine, for he's often in the gutter
Though he never gives a sign!

His clothes are old and tattered
But it doesn't really matter, walking on
His lonely ways, through a thousand lonely days;
There's a Luger deep inside him with a trigger
Like a hair, and the only one to pull it
Is the one who put it there…

19 March 1971

That Light - That Sound

'I've noticed that light before,' she said,
'In the pale of the dawn
In a passing storm,
In the eyes of a child having fun;
In the stories I'm told
In the glitter of gold
In the habit of many a nun.'

'I've noticed that sound before,' she said,
'In the tinkle of glass
In the whisper of grass
In the ring of an ambulance bell;
In the patter of rain
In a whimper of pain
In the secrets that children tell.'

18 May 1971

My Love-2

Armourless fool to emotion I am
And to think that I really believed I was strong
And immune to such things,
        such an arrogant man
Who can feel himself free of involvement!
Let the world roll along
In deception and lies,
Let the stories be murmured afar,
Let my name be defamed

And be run through the mire,
I'll continue to follow my star.

A man is a complex of loving and hate,
Neither can wait,
                his permanent state,
Though I would have thought that
A love that was strong would be
Welcomed by any and all;
It's never the way,
                the hypocrites say
What they will just to see a man fall.

What's wrong, what is right,
The darkness of night and your touch
                are the comfort I need,
Two people in bed are defenceless, it's said,
The cold shell of armour is already shed
                on the floor where it lies
With the coldness of days spent in
                unloving actions
With people and factions,
Avoiding the causes and hate-filled abstractions
That tear love apart at the source.

In loving and love there's a light from above
That protects from the hurt of a lie,
In love there's no wrong,
So as in a song
                we go hopefully on with a sigh.

5 July 1971

1895 Flashlight Society

I've founded a club for our frustrated poets
Whose thoughts and ideas are not too well read,
Whose visions are flashes that light up the mind
For the instant they rattle along in your head.
They write in the garrets of cobweb-filled houses
Sit wearily passing a pen through a page,
And see by the light of those same dying flashes
That bring on the visions of transported mediums,
Calling up Spirits that quarrel and rage.

The Flashlight Society meets in the cellar
And sparkles in silence away through the night,
They dress in the style of the turn of the century,
Try to evoke all the sense and the style of the gentry
Who faltered and fell in the fight.
Who fell in the onslaught of motor cars rolling,
Who dropped at the sight of an aircraft in flight,
Who gave up their poetry reading and literature,
Sadly relinquished their art, and their culture
Was lost as they finally dropped out of sight.

For soon was the world to be filled with mechanics
Who fiddled with paintwork and gleaming machines,
Who, rapt in the art of their growing technology
Surging ahead in the pride of invention were
Losing the art of enjoying their dreams.
For all they could read were the newspaper funnies
And technical journals with pictures to suit,
With radio newscasts to keep them informed of the
Latest events that they could not refute.

Poets were swallowed in industry's labour
To sweat out the poetry nobody penned,
But still were a few of them, scribbled in silence
In hopes that the sickness would finally mend.
On through their sons and the sons of their sons
They have waited forever to speak of their plight,
The Flashlight Society's weaving its dreams
On a tapestry woven of letters and light.

Sometimes I sit in the cobwebs and dust
And I read and I drift on the muse of a line,
Watching creations of pen-bitten visions
Like artistic artifacts swelling and growing
In beauty and charm that will always be mine.
Poe would be proud of the Flashlight Society
Striving to bring out their dreams to the fore,
Let a man read of it, let a man need of it,
Welcome he is at Society's door.

Tell me the story of Benjamin's glory
Who fought at the battle of Eljamin Flood,
Read me the way that the brave Euphidores
Had gained him a wife who was covered in blood.
Tell me of Turquoise and Marble and Miracles,
Honour in dying and Victory's joy,
Stir me within with the tales of the brave
And the head of a foe, or a child with a toy.

Let me forget that I live in the seventies
Hustle and bustle and tension and pace,
Let me remember the best that our fathers
As children would read of the best of the race.
Patriotism is dead for the present

But poetry brings it all back with a rush,
When the Society breaks through the bottleneck
Holding their visions in permanent check,
Maybe we'll see all the jaded in line
For the dreams that will take them
                                away from the crush.
For dream weavers soon will be high in demand,
A queue for a dream of a minute or so,
While songs are repeating their time-hardened melodies,
Saddened and soulful and sickening parodies,
Poetry takes them in tow.

Sound is the sound of a woman in labour
But noise is the noise of the damned,
Industry's noises are drowning the sounds
Of the man and his love for the land.
But while we are rushing toward the abyss
Of the lost and a terrible war,
And slavery then for the few that survive
In the visions the prophets saw,
The Flashlight Society's work will survive
On the damp of a mouldy shelf,
'Til one day we're able to throw off the chains
Of a civilization that's lost in its aims
And the heir to the fortune in paper and verse
Will then add to the visions himself.

20 July 1971

Corporal Corporal

Corporal Corporal
Finally made it
He don't have to struggle no more,
Fought the good fight since the Army began
And it don't really matter which war.

Corporal Corporal
Bullied his men and
Pushed on with the rape of the land,
Marched on his stomach from Moscow to Gettysburg
Never extending his hand.

Corporal Corporal
Silently thought of
A God who would march at his side,
It helped when his conscience would start to annoy him
Or one of the Officers died.

Corporal Corporal
Spoke of his duty
To country, to God and to King,
But never would speak of his duty to kill
Because that was a secondary thing!

Corporal Corporal
As you retreat
Do you think that your God's at your side,
He left you in shame at such animal cruelty,
Damned you for arrogant pride!

Corporal Corporal
Finally made it
He don't have to struggle no more,
Listened just once to his conscience and blew out
His brains on the lavatory floor!

21 July 1971

A Letter To My Son

I hope, one day, you'll read this, son,
Long long since this was penned,
On this I've thought for many a day, your
Very best of friends. Now you may think that
Every now and then I was a touch too harsh,
May God, who is the greatest judge, reach down and touch
Your heart of hearts, and let you know my many parts.
With prayer I entered fatherhood
In trepidation for my youth, and
Fortune smiled when you arrived, your
Every cry, a cry of truth.

I've watched you grow, I've watched you play, a
Little lad whose smiles are like the rainbows
On a winter's day, a balm to soothe my cares away. A
Violent world I brought you to and
Each of us must feel his way, but if
You need a helping hand, remember mine was
On your arm, if only until yesterday when
Under providence's care you crossed a
Road without my hand.

Maybe when I'm old and grey you'll call me
Old man, stupid, fool;
Then I'll know I've overstayed.
Happiness is seeing you today and
Every other day, so if we're torn apart for now
Remember that I didn't chose to be away from you this way.

I hope to have so many years of
Love and understanding, as we stroll beside each
Other in this scheme of things we didn't plan.
Vexing though this life may be, let's try to grasp and
                                      understand
Each other's problems as they rise.
Yes, my son, we'll fight at times, we'll argue
On, we'll sing a song, we'll throw a punch
                                    and always miss, just
Understand, I love you, boy, I love you – only this!

6 September 1971

Peace On Earth

'Come on Jim, we'll earn a bob,
I'm feelin' good, at peace;
The sort'a thing a chap don't say
On any uvver day.
It's Christmas Eve, 'n Dad's gorn out,
'E's taken Muvver bowlin',
They'll come 'ome tiddled up as well
'N probly raise up merry 'ell,
So I'm fer Carol Singing.'

'Ave you gorn orf yer 'ead ole mate,
I ain't a kid no more yer know,
I'm neely twelve, well, in a munf,
An' I ain't 'ad no bleedin' lunch.
This singin' never gets yer nowt
You know that all too well.'
'Oh, don't be such a misry guts,
We'll stand a chance o' pies 'n chestnuts
Up on Nobby 'ill.'

The woman glanced down at the rags
And wrinkled up her powdered nose
As Christmas lights winked on and off
And all the boys could do was cough.
'For God's sake, go away,' and slam...
'You rotten...'
'No - don't say it, Jim,
It's Christmas Eve, remember Him!'
'Oh yeah, what's comin' over Tim?
You never gave a damn.'

'Yer wrong there Jim, I care fer 'im,
I care fer what 'e did.
Fer jus' one night, let's stick it out,
Sing softer tho', try not ter shout.
There mus' be one ter pay the price,
There's allwus one ter shoot the dice,
The money's 'ere, I've 'eard Dad say
There's them that throws it all away,
So jus' sing soft 'n nice.'

'Clear off you brats, don't scrounge round here
A man can't have a quiet beer...'

'Please go, or I shall call the police…'
('ere Tim, d'yer see that luscious piece?)
'You little swine, clear off I said,
A man can't even go to bed…'
Clear off, begone, slam, and the rest,
They'd turned away before she had
A chance to say - 'Come in…
I've pies and nuts and lemonade,
Mince pies and drink, a perfect brew…'
And Tim blinked back a tear or two.

'Ere, this is nice, 'n thank you Mam…'
But Tim just couldn't speak at all,
He smiled and ate, and drank and smiled
And hung his head, and felt quite small.
'Here's half a crown for each of you,
Now keep it up… He's listening,
And don't you think to harshly of
The ones who don't invite you in.'

'Now that's what Christmas means,' said Jim,
'I love 'er mate, I really do,
Wiv 'er around now, life's worf livin','
And Tim had nodded too.
'Now 'ere's a lark, we've got five bob
An'… Hey! Jus' what d'yer think yer at?'
But Tim had turned, was coming back;
'You dropped yer coin in that bloke's 'at.'

'I know, just 'ave a look at 'im,
'E's seen a Christmas Day or two,
Yer think we're tatty, look at 'im,
'E's much worse off than me or you.

You said yer loved that woman there,
She makes a spark o' life worf livin',
This Christmas thing, it seems ter me
Is not fer takin', it's fer givin'.'

Jim stood there stunned, and bit his lip,
'I 'ate ter say yer right again…'
Then made his way toward the chap
Who stood and watched him, wondering.
'Ere mate, a merry Christmas Day,
Nar don't you fritter it away…'
And left the man, eyes glistening
To run back to his tiny Tim.
'Yer know, ole mate, this is the thing,
This Peace on Earth,
     Goodwill ter men!'

13 December 1971

The Seven Winds

My mother's folk were miners,
My father's folk were kings,
But my folk were sailor folk
Who rode the seven winds.

My father's race was thoroughbred
My mother's race was proud,
But my race is a mongrel race
That stood astride the world.

As fishermen they spread their nets
To catch the rising tide,
But caught themselves an Empire
In folly, and in pride.

For some had sailed from Portsmouth,
And some had sailed from Hull,
And some had sailed from Tiger Bay
To follow the seaborne gull.

And some had died in tempest,
In wrecks on the Spanish Main,
They turned about and beat it out
Then beat it back again.

And I... I sailed from London Town
To catch the seven winds,
For my mother's folk were miners
And my father's folk were kings.

And when I die, in field afar,
Away from my native land,
My soul will turn and beat it out
Then beat it back again.

My mother's folk were miners,
My father's folk were kings,
But my folk were sailor folk
Who rode the seven winds.

15 December 1971

Borth

You ask me, where would I wish to lie
When this life has done with me,
When the deed is done and the battle won,
Or lost, as the case may be,
When my heart is full in the race to ride
And my eyes have drunk their fill,
Then take me back to the land I loved
In the days I yearn for still.

For there I'll live once more the days
Of a carefree, laughing child,
I'll smell the new-baked morning bread
And remember how we smiled,
I'll hear the sea come thundering in
Its tide upon the land,
And there, with the grace of the lord above,
I'll hold my father's hand.

I'll see my mother as she was,
Lord how the years have flown,
Her hair the colour of shepherd's dawn,
The Welsh will know their own,
My sister, close as we were, but now,
We may well be again,
When the tide of life has passed us by
And our moon is on the wane.

My brother's first few faltering steps
Were taken along the sand,
Many's the memory he enjoys
Of a green and beautiful land.

Though we both set off for the outside track
To carry our swags so free,
It's nice to pause on a winter's day
To stroll through a memory.

Remember the squawk of the sea-bound gulls
And the sharp, salt tang of the sea,
And the cliff-top farm, and the attic barn
And the calf named after me?
Where the monument looked out over all
On the Aberwennel side,
And the stream that must be flowing still
With the cliff so close beside.

You ask me, where would I wish to lie
When this life has done with me?
Just take me back from the outside track
And over the heaving sea,
Then drive me on through the countryside
'Til you see the coast of Wales,
And look for Borth, where the children laugh
And the old men swill their ales,
Where the sea meets up with the sandy shore
And the soaring seagulls scream,
I'll take my rest of the race to ride
And find my childhood dream.

26 December 1971

-1972-

Brother Love

I knelt to peer at my brother's face
In the light of the early morn,
The face of the man I'd grown to love
Since the day we both were born,
And I watched a passer-by shake his head
And quietly walk away
As my heart was stilled with a fearful thought,
So still my brother lay;
And the lights shone out through the scattered trees
Where the blood-drawn ghouls were stood,
And I felt the pain in the morning rain
Where the car lay on its hood.

But something stirred in the tangled wreck
And my brother's eyes were wide,
'Forgive me, John, but I'm almost gone,'
He said, in a sad aside.
'Just tell me, how is the girl you saw,
Thrown out as we hit the tree,
I'd turn my head if I didn't know
It would be the end of me.'
'She's right,' I said, 'just a cut or two,'
And bit my nail to the quick,
To glance at the shape beyond the trees
That lay with a broken neck.

'Don't worry, mate, we'll get you out,
There's only a slight delay.'

I faltered then, and I almost cried,
He seemed so far away;
And blood was thick on his face and hair,
His breath was coming fast,
I prayed to God and the stars above
And I cursed myself at the last.
To be so powerless, kneeling there,
My brother and friend to save,
And he caught up in the throes of death
With a twisted car his grave.

'You wonder who she could be,' he said,
And twisted his face to smile,
'My own sweet love, and her name is Jan,'
He said, in a little while.
'And I know you think I'm a crazy fool
With a wife as good as mine…'
And I thought he was, but I didn't say
And I gave no outward sign.
'But I love my wife, I really do…
I love them both the same!
For the sake of the children, keep your peace,'
For the sake of their mother's name.'

I glanced at Jan in the gathering dawn
And I saw she'd found her peace,
And the tears sprang into my brother's eyes
As he sensed his love's release.
'So she's gone,' he sobbed in a broken cry
And the twisted metal clung,
As his head lay out through the open door
In the tragedy of the young.
But the fading light from the morning star

Shone back from my brother's eyes,
And I shivered there as I held his hand
In the wake of my feeble lies.

'Don't blame the girl, don't blame my wife,
It's I and the world to blame,
My love's not kept in a mantle jar
It's an ever-burning flame.
We've been so happy in other days
Whenever the world was free,
I fell asleep at the wheel tonight
To dream of the open sea,
To dream of the days we brothers shared
In the carefree bloom of youth,
When all we built were our memories,
And sought for the burning truth.'

'We sought for the burning truth,' he smiled,
'Far better we'd let it be,
The truth can ruin the ones we love,
The truth has ruined me.
But kiss the kids for their Daddy's sake
And say that I'm called away,
And if they ask, I love them all,
You'll know what it's best to say…
Love was my only stock in trade,'
He said, in a voice so weak,
And died, as the sun rose slowly up
And the tears rolled down my cheek.

5 March, 1972

Afterword on the Book of Life

I dripped my blood on the final word
To give it a mark of mine,
And show that the words you've read tonight
Are the words of a bloody time.
If you think I'm bitter and broken up
And the title's only a lure,
Then read it again in the Sydney Sun
And go for the total cure.

You read the book on a whim, you say,
You'd never have picked it up,
You feel you've drunk from a brackish spring
The words from an empty cup,
But watch the faces of tiny girls
Who die in the madman's spell,
Or bear the scar of their tiny lives
To grow to an empty shell.

The cure has given you nought, you say,
Or nothing that wasn't known,
Only the thoughts that you didn't need
As you sat on your thoughtless throne.
A cure is only of use to those
Who know that there's something wrong,
So why did you open the title page,
And why did you carry on?

If all I've done is to underline
The things you already knew,
Or touched you once in a tender spot
That started a tear in you,

Or drawn you out in a sympathy
You swore you'd lost for good,
I've done all I ever meant to do…
And all that I thought I could.

15 March, 1972

Stirrup Cup

Why is it always a summer's day
Or the shades of spring in the old years hay
And never a winter's night, I say.

Why is a man a drunken fool
To be used by drink as a Satan tool
Not seeing the depth of the drowning pool.

Where is the hand, and where the eyes
Brought to shame with the sad goodbyes
And all for the one who thought him wise.

But sorrow only belongs to those
Who give of themselves in another's clothes
To break the heart of the one that knows.

It's all been said and sung before
The broken heart at the open door
And never a smile for evermore.

Life is the everflowing stream,
Love is the hurt we thought to dream
To plague ourselves with a might-have-been.

14 April 1972

Apologia

All my life was laid to waste the
Night I wrote to you in haste, unseeing
In the spell of what was best,
But sorrow and a wild regret will
Never change the wisdom of it, wisdom
That will bring me little rest.

But have you heard yourself say no to the
Very thing you wanted so, and
Knowing it would only bring you scorn.
But powerless to step aside for the
Very thing you sought to hide
Was written-in, the day that you were born.

The victims of an astral game where
Cruel adds are put to shame and
Life and love are cheap among the stakes,
The roulette wheel will clatter on, upsetting
Men when we are gone, another player
Cries as he awakes!

So ours is just to reminisce those memories
That brought us bliss, and nevermore
To see them come again,
To think back on those holy days, before
We went our separate ways, and so
Discovered how to suffer pain.

The truth is but the blackest lie when heeding
Truth can make you cry, so say goodbye

To truth and try to smile,
Do you recall, of course you do, the day that
One was made of two, the day we tried
Our conscience to beguile.

We should have halted, there and then, but we
Just carried on again and shut our eyes
To consequence and such,
The days were filled with sheer delight, the
Nights were pools of candlelight, and half
Our world of sense was that of touch.

The clowning in the parks and greens, the
Happiness, the stormy scenes when
Everything was vital to the plot,
The times you shed those bitter tears will
Turn and haunt me through the years, as like as
Will your love, as like as not.

As once we journeyed to the tip, in fun
And for the hell of it, to scavenge
Anything we saw of note,
We journey now the road apart and
Bleed a little from the heart, reciting
All we were, as if by rote.

And now I lie awake at night recalling
Your sweet face to sight, reliving
All the best I found in you,
Your patience with my way-out schemes,
Ill tempers, and fantastic dreams, and
Always loving, honest, good and true.

It may be that this mortal span is

Just enough to cripple man and
Smash him down in fortune's stinging rack,
But were I offered any more, in hell
Or heaven, peace or war, I'd use it all
To give your loving back.

14 April 1972

Red Sky Warning

I saw the cloud in the morning sky
So I turned to go back inside,
And I said to my wife, 'It's a shepherd's dawn,
Or the red sky early warning, torn
By the man with the evil eye.'

The silence hung in a leaden pall
As she turned her face away,
And I said: 'I'm only the man behind,
I'm not to account for all mankind
Or a cloud at the break of day.'

She looked again and she pulled the blind
And the house was dark and still.
'I've looked my last on the works of man
Through whispered tears on a trembling hand,
Or the cloud beyond the hill.'

So she sat herself where she sits today
By the glow of the ash-wood fire,
But she sees and hears and tells me nought
While the devil inside her can't be bought,
Or ever be made to tire.

So whenever a cloud in the early dawn
Glows red in the morning sky,
I say to my wife: 'It's a shepherd's dawn,
Or the red sky early warning, torn
By the man with the evil eye!'

9 June 1972

Mary Boots

(Beloved wife of Charles M. Boots, died... 1898 aged 23 years)

Where have you gone to, Mary Boots,
Where do your tresses lie?
This weed and thorn your grave has borne
To halt my passing by.

Where is the song of Mary Boots,
When did you wine and dine,
And live and love with the stars above,
And cry with your eyes a-shine?

What did you die of, Mary Boots,
Death in the bloom of youth,
Your cheek so cold in the morning gold,
Your eyes, the sparkling truth.

Where is your memoir, Mary Boots,
Crumbling sand and stone,
The wind and rain, and the weed again
May soon leave you alone.

10 June 1972

The Only Way to Win

I've said before that I'd like to go
In the clash and the grate of gears,
Not a lingering death in the early spring
In a room of a thousand tears,
But a leap of light on a winter's night
The scream of a speed machine,
That last long terrible, deadly thrill
And a curse with my eyes a-gleam.
From a mountain road in the murk and mist
With never a soul to say:
'He looked like a man in a crazy dream
With the Devil and all to pay',
Or rapping it out on a Besa twin
To the top, or over the ton,
And taking a dive on the ocean road
In the early morning sun!

It's ever the way of the working man
Who toils and swears unblest,
To let his brass and his sorrows fall
On a less than virgin breast,
To take a whore to the razz-matazz
Of the local city scene,
And never enquire as she jazzes off
With whom, or where she's been,
But lives for money and lives for kicks
And lives for a drunken spree,
And lives for the day the Eagle spits,
And lives for the used to be.

For the used to be and the might have been
And the could be, even still,
If the lottery picks the in-between
Or the jockey makes a kill,
But the years roll on and a thousand dreams
Despair in the morning light,
And the hopes and schemes are laid to rest
In the everlasting night,
And a mind that tires of the constant debt
Slips off to its own retreat,
In a frigid flat with a
Frigid wife on little downhill street,
For the only joy is the chrome machine
That sits outside the door,
That gathers dust and the neighbour's lust
And a monthly bill, (for sure).

The poor get poor and the rich get rich
In the way that it's always been,
For I've never seen a poor man rich
Or a rich man in-between,
And the only everlasting life
For the working man today,
Is the everlasting overdraft,
And the everlasting pay,
For only the rich can afford to buy
Their way to the Pearly Gates,
While the rest of us must scrimp
And steal, and save for the water rates,
Though I still believe, oh I still believe
In a God that's just and fair,
I only ask if he gave us up
Or turned and left us here?

God be good to my overdraft and
Help me along the way,
Well, what do you want from a working man,
Just what did I oughter say?
What did my kids 'ave done to you
To merit their lives ahead,
A fight and a scramble for lousy jobs
And the coin for their daily bread,
We don't get manna from heaven now
As they did in the days of old,
And the meek that inherit the earth today
Can only be paid in gold!
So give me a ride on a Bonneville
Or a drag on a Besa twin,
And I'll take it up to the mountain top
In the only way to win!

23 June 1972

My Generation – 39/45

Out of the nightmare came a dream,
Out of the night, the dawn,
A thousand bombers overhead
The night that I was born...
The world was filled with glistening eyes
And broken up with sorrow...
I heard the bombers overhead
And in the dream, the bombers said
    'We're over here to strike you dead
    Or turn your head, tomorrow!'

Always I heard the bombers' words
Echoing through my mind,
They still return, although the journey
Left them far behind.
The world gave out a terrible groan
To see the saddest day…
I heard them say: 'It must be so
The babes reap what the parents sow,
    They'll tread where we would fear to go
    But never know the way.'

The stars of war were stars of mine
The day that I was born,
You wonder why we're so disturbed,
It's written in the dawn.
The world was sat with a bleeding head
And broken up with sorrow…
I know the ragged mile we've led
Is based upon the drone that said:
    'We're over here to strike you dead
    Or turn your head, tomorrow!'

19 July 1972

The Axiom

In Chantris Lane I caught a glimpse
Of someone through a window pane,
Distorted by the defects and
The frosted glass effect,
And there I learnt an axiom
That most escapes the common man,
Through bigotry, short-sightedness,
And often plain neglect!

In Chantris Lane the one I saw
Was someone I had seen before,
So well I knew the culprit was
The frosted window pane,
But tongues will slander he and she
To bring the greatest misery
Before we find those tongues are but
The frosted glass again!

6 August 1972

Coming Home

My mind is musty, overgrown
With weeds and deeds the years have sown
And names untold that never left a face,
I turned to you to find you'd gone
Just like the bird that nodded on
Unknowing, and unseeing in its grace.

But must the world of you and I
Take such a breath of time to die
We hungered for the far horizon race,
I turned to find the years between
Had spun the web, but lost the dream;
The far horizons stare us in the face!

9 September 1972

Come Quickly

Before the mountains
Quake and fall away,
And rivers dry, or
Turn to scattered clay,
Could I live to see the day
          Come Quickly!

Before the headstrong
Drown themselves in blood
And armies fall, or
Choke in lakes of mud,
When all is lost in fire and flood
          Come Quickly!

Before the hopeful few
Are sick at heart
And die forlorn, or
Torn from soul apart,
Unknowing when to stop or start
          Come Quickly!

Before the hunter's
Stopped and overawed
And comes to take the foolish
At their word,
Could I redeem myself, Oh Lord
        Come Quickly!

9 October 1972

Skyjacker

It won't do you any good
Though you never thought it would,
For a man is quite the sum of all his deeds,
And although the quest for glory
Rates a medal in the story
All it rates in life is death, and widow's weeds.

'How could you philosophize
Say you're worldly, and you're wise,
When you've never known the heartache of the few?
Have you never heard of causes,
Read the pain between the pauses
Or do you believe the propaganda view?'

'I believe a man must do
What his conscience prompts him to,
But his deeds should not affect the uninvolved.
You may live, or go out fighting
But the cause you're underwriting
Will be left to other people, unresolved.'

'That may be the truth of it
Though a man may never sit
And ignore the facts that influence his life;
He may hope, and go on praying
But such tactics are delaying
And the time will come; he'll have to turn the knife.'

'So you turn the knife on those
Who have nothing to oppose,
There's a hundred faultless people on this plane,
Would you see so many dying
For the freedom you're denying...'
'There are thousands in my country - who's to blame?'

So the pilot bowed his head
Flew the course that he had said
And they landed in the early morning sun,
But the skyjacker was dying
By the time the pilot, flying, said:
'You never solve a problem with a gun!'

12 October 1972

This is the Way

As I recall, when we were young
And life the refrain of a song, unsung,
We'd walk in the glare of the winter white
And dream sweet dreams,
     sweet dreams at night.

And many's the time that I've seen you fall
And hurt so much that you hurt us all;
Ah, those were the days that were lost and won,
When we were young,
    when we were young.

But now, with families of our own
It's hard to believe how the years have flown
For still we struggle from day to day
But half a world
    And a world away.

And still we stagger, and still we fall,
And still the hurt will hurt us all
For these are the days that are lost and won
And this is the way
The song is sung…

13 October 1972

Byron Bay

I lay a-dream in Byron Bay
And felt a voice to sigh and say:
'Get up, get up,
There's much to be done,
And more to be seen, to be worked at and won.'

Her eyes were sparkling pools of gold
Her hair a glittering tale, untold,
'Get up, get on,'
She seemed to say,
But whispered her wisdom and wishes away

'Don't lie in an idle content, replete,
Be stirring your imagery, stirring your feet,
Get on, get out
And conjure the ebb
Of a moonbeam laced with a spider's web.'

I smiled to notice the voice so fine
A bubbling nectar, a sparkling wine,
'Be still, desist,
I taste the content
Of an April dawn the creator lent.'

'Conjure me flowers a yard across
And gossamer flights of the Albatross,
Awake, look out,
The faerie spell,
Adrift in the midst of a wishing well!'

'How could I conjure a looking-glass?
A poet is merely a man, alas!'
'Just turn, and see
In mortal guise
The enchanted dawn through a faerie's eyes!'

I looked around for the barest glimpse
Of a sight seen neither before, nor since;
'Be soft, be still
I dream all day
Of my Faerie Queene of Byron Bay.'

16 October 1972

Death of an Airman

(In memory of Cpl. Gus Brittain, Townsville, Qld.)

Abis, Ackerman, Benson and Blunt,
Stand to attention and look to the front,
Chiswell and Barnett
Who told you to fall out,
You'd think this was bush week
Or a Boy Scout Camp call-out;
Get back into line or I might have you all out
Tonight…
Did you hear what I said to you, Argent?'

> *'But there's a man dying on the tarmac, Sergeant!'*

'I never liked Wednesdays,' declaimed Sergeant Black,
'Too soon to go forward, too late to go back!
Dexter and Dooley
I'll have your attention,
I'm not calling names
For an honourable mention,
I'll charge the whole bunch for a spark of presumption
Tomorrow…
I'll tell you once more, *Mister* Argent…

> *'But there's a man, dying on the tarmac, Sergeant!'*

'Haven't you seen a man faint before?
Harris and Jenkins
Block up that four!
Fill up the gap that your mate has relinquished
We'll count him as present, but almost extinguished,'

The Sergeant guffawed, in attempts to distinguish
Himself...
Now what in creation d'you want with me, Argent?'

   'A man has just died on the tarmac, Sergeant!'

24 October 1972

Scene From A Yamaha

Scene from a Yamaha
Dry wind at dawning,
Scatter leaves steeplewards
Hayrick, reborn in,
Sleepy-eyed quarry stone
Quail stride between,
Such have I never known...
Such have I seen.

Cockcrow at Biddeford
Peppercorn to Willow,
What breaks the still and sweet
Summerset in silo,
Field mouse to Yamaha
What have you seen?
Sigh echoes back again...
Dream the sweet dream!

16 November 1972

Pen & Ink

If all the world were pen and ink
And all the folk were sorrow,
If all the trees were burly breeze
And Wednesdays, come tomorrow,
If all the stars were out of sight
And snow fell softly overnight,
If all we woke to morning white
Who'd lantern light the morrow?

If all the earth were beaten gold
And all the fields were fallow,
If all the bees were try-to-please
And all the mud marshmallow,
If all the children walked away
To never change from day to day
But gambolled in the autumn hay,
Who'd taper light the tallow?

29 November 1972

How Many Men

How many men march, tramp
By the marshlight, tell tall tales
By the willow and pine,
Such fine pillow-wine caught in a light-
Ray, daylight catch-cry homeward sway,
Whisper in the wind, wash-whisper away.

How many mouths lie, make
Sigh-sound say, truth to tell
To who knows who?
So few listen, glisten-eye in the Moon-
Light, restless rove in the track black nights,
Sounds of the soldiers sadness sights!

30 December 1972

-1973-

1972

'Will someone buy this year of mine?
A year, knocked down to first bid...'
I watched the old man through the wine
To know well what he did...

'A twelvemonth worth no more than this,
With all its sorrows, all its bliss?'

'Ah... such a year is ours to give
   Now it's done...
They'll say:

   'That year did poets live...'

            God Bless Everyone!

1 January 1973

Saturn in the 10th

So these old grey bones are dead, Saturn,
Resting my weary head,
And your dreaded fall has swept over all
For that's what your prophet said.

But the fall was long ago, Saturn,
Shine with your blighted ray,
For you'll not stir me, nor the words you see
If you shine 'til your dying day.

Though you shine 'til the Sun burns dim, Saturn,
I've earned this brief respite,
For I stand or fall by the words I scrawled
While my eyes could see the light.

12 February 1973

Starling

Wild winter bird, your same old graces,
Check and charm familiar faces, mine
To hide a heartbreak, healing,
Steal a kiss that's not worth stealing,

Starling!

Fly, flutter back to back street bolsters,
Cool white sheets of youngsters, oldsters,
See the cloud tuft sky, grey scarring,
Dare one now so long past daring,

Darling!

Sing winter wine, of mine and merry,
Lips red-run, sweet juice of berry, vine
That clings, she said, sad carlin,
Love the love that's lost, my darling,

Starling!

19 February 1973

The Venus Bird

What does she want, the Venus Bird,
Tip of the tyrant's tongue,
Beat of the heart that barely stirs
Sip of the song, unsung,
Soul of the loved, unwanted one.

Where does she go, the Venus Bird
Drifts in a cobweb sigh,
Settles in silks and velvet dreams
The spark of a lover's eye,
Or waits for the mood to pass her by.

What does she do, the Venus Bird,
Cry at the morning tide,
Wave to her love at the open door,
Such emptiness inside,
The Venus Bird once more denied.

21 April 1973

And...

and when you were a young girl
with dreams in the night skies and
passionate strangers were following your sighs,
you just wished for a vivid red
double-decker bus on the Causo, and a
teddy bear in velvet but
six feet alive...
    (and a silk skirt uplifted
      while annointing your thighs).

...and your friends were giggle girls
arrayed in gym tunics with
crayons for scribble words on lavatory walls,
with gauche legs for the teachers,
flash-flashing down the corridors
and gash-red lips waiting for the
mother of pearl...
    (and a love pit never ending
      at the end of the world).

...and your sighs were bubble sighs
for the sharp-shooting larrikins
and your thighs were trouble thighs
that worried sad men,
and your cries were wild cries
from the red eyes of the sunset
when the world seemed so empty
in the dim days of then...
    (when your love took to another girl
      and never came again).

...and you gaze past the pram hood
at the young girls laugh-laughing and
run, skip and jumping to pull at their hair,
and there's sadness in the memory
as your feet ache in the market
and you wish now for a daisy
to plait in your hair...
    (and you feel the life within you
      in an empty despair).

23 May 1973

And...Pt. II

...and when you were a lover
With your star-spangled bright eyes
In the heart-breaking knowledge
That he'd do you no wrong,
You thought like some Madonna
In the white light of the morning
And your heart was so very tender
With his sing-along song...
    (but it took more than a singer
      to sing you along).

...and when you were a mother
in the chill of a bitter winter
and cold hands came grasping
to feel for your warmth,
you cried for the body yearnings
that felt for your offspring
and clawed them to your shelter
in the depths of the storm...

    (and you wondered in the darkness
     had they ever been born).

…and when I wake you early
in the midst of a sugar-sweet dream
and you raise your soft lips
to be given, or take;
you moan like the wind westerly,
sough-soughing in the treetops,
and you move like the kestrel
long musing mistake…
    (and you claw like the whippet whirlwind
     clutch-claw wide awake).

…and when you are a statue
in the bright sheen of the full moon,
while shiver-out evenings
come holding my hand,
you never hear strange voices
but premonitions take you
to wrap you in velvet
and bury you in sand…
    (for the voice that will never reach you
     is the voice of a man).

17 June 1973

And…Pt. III

…and when you were a seesaw
in the grip of an old dilemma
while unloved ones ranted and stormed the Bastille,
you wrapped your head in feather-down

and shivered in fever
for you only knew where
your body had been...
    (and once, you said you loved me
    in the midst of a dream).

...and when you cried out in
your total abandon
to wonder why I never cried aloud too,
I mentioned that Venus
and Neptune were rising,
but never so fast or so
far as we do...
    (and you turned your back towards me
    as your brown eyes turned blue).

...and why do we fight in
the way of the loveless
you said to me once on a bright afternoon,
for such is the nature of
water and sodium,
or Scorpio and Venus
or Mars and the Moon;
    (or life's fickle fortunes
    inscribed on the rune).

...and deep in your chart there's
the whisper of a twinkle
in your bright eyes, and a chuckle that forces a smile,
and a giggle that you stifled
in the sad-solemn girl-face
but nurtured in the woman
in the happy glowtime;

(and my hands bear your pleasure
   oh woman of mine).

…and when you were a young girl
with dreams in the night skies and
passionate strangers were following your sighs,
you just wished for a vivid red
double-decker bus on the Causo, and a
teddy bear in velvet, but
six feet alive…
    (and a silk skirt uplifted
     while anointing your thighs).

29 July 1973

Castle Walls

She ventured out from her castle walls
 In hopes of meeting me,
I said: 'we'll flee to the furthest shores,
We'll run to the far countree,
We'll sit in bliss on a grassy slope
To see our love returned;'
I looked again at the moat and saw
That all the boats were burned.

'How shall I leave my castle walls
And all that keeps me free,
I fear the step that you wish to take
Could spell the end for me,
I wish to come, if I only dared,'
She said in a sad reply,
The moat was still and the air was chill
And the moon was riding high.

I stood alone by the castle moat
As she turned to seek the warm;
'The roads of life are a trap,' I cried,
'But so is a thunderstorm,
So are the walls of a castle when
The mortar turns to dust,
So are the bolts on a castle gate
When the hinges start to rust.'

'You weary me, I must be free,'
The tower echoed, black,
'As free as the castle walls allow,'
I called in sadness back.
'It's not too late for the grassy slope
To see our love returned -'
I looked again at the moat and saw
That all the boats were burned.

12 July 1973

Winterspray

It's cold and damp in the light of day
The birds are gaunt, and tall and grey,
I walk the line to the sound of my mind
And the wind that clatters away…
I should be sad for I never know
Why the feeling sweeps me over so,
But ever a breeze will come my way
Like a breath of you in the winterspray.

The countryside is a green, they say

That you only see in the month of May,
The beat of mine is a bitumen line,
Of black, and a murky grey.
The wind whips eddies of powder rain
To the haunting sound of an old refrain,
And many's the thought that, day by day
I have of you in the winterspray.

1971

Half Remembered

We touch things we see not
And know things we know not
And dream of sweet things that
We've not set in store,
We say things we think not
And do things we do not
And wonder at wonders
We've wondered before.

I see you in shades of
Another life's colours
Where sweetness and pleasance
And love was the play,
Where green was the colour
You wore to the wedding
That bound me to see where
Your loveliness lay.

And wild was the country
We took for our mansion,
And green was the valley

And green were your eyes,
And seen were you riding
So high in the saddle
Of Pacer and Gracer
By Barking Wood rise.

I vaguely see visions
Of cottagers doorsteps
In winter-white mantles
Of featherdown snow,
And you looking on me
While glowing with love-light
As I took you on to
The valley below.

And sometimes I see when
I laid you in velvet
And stole a last kiss from
The lips we had shared,
And went on to mourn 'til
The tides took my eyesight,
And left me to wonder how
Much you had cared.

Now when I awake with
These visions so fleeting
That fade and recede in
The glow of the dawn,
I look at you lying so
Peaceful beside me
And smile at the love shared
Before we were born.

We touch things we see not

And know things we know not
And dream of sweet things that
We've not set in store,
We say things we think not
And do things we do not
And wonder at wonders
We've wondered before…

21 August 1973

Nightcaller

May you ply your trade in the morning,
In the dark of the early hours,
May you walk your way to the break o' day
'Til the pride, or the spirit sours,
With special times for the quiet ones
Too shy to walk right in;
Who only have need of a woman's touch
When the world outside is much to much,
So ask if you'll let them in.

And you let them in to your body,
And you give them animal warmth,
And you give them the heart to go out again
To brave the animal storm;
But you lie with eyes unseeing
In the deed that must be done,
For never a man will turn your head
If you've possibly seen him before, in bed,
Or think he's a lonely one.

So you ply your trade in the morning

By the light of the breaking dawn,
And you've had your fill of the dingy rooms
Or the back of the neighbour's lawn,
And the city's awake, and stirring,
As you drift so weary home;
To the cheerless air of your city flat
(With its cupboards, bare as the welcome mat),
To sleep, but quite alone.

28 August 1973

The Deepest Cut

Have ever you looked and seen the smile
I hold inside for you,
Or caught the glow of the candlelight
I keep reflected too,
I've heard it said that a man can keep
His feelings locked in lies,
But truth shines out in a thousand ways
From the lovelight in his eyes.

I'd never have let you see the soul
I bare so shamelessly,
If I hadn't been caught so unprepared
As I wandered aimlessly,
I found myself in an empty room
Locked out of your vacant stare.
Drinking the essence of cinnamon wine
And the scent of your fragrant hair.

It's ever the way of love, sweet love,
To take a man aback,
To bring on home to the emptiness
Fulfilment sadly lacked,
But the deepest cut is the certainty
That after the first surprise,
He'll never put out of his mind again
The truth in a woman's eyes.

8 September 1973

To Lie in a Caravan

Driving in starlight
The day long behind us,
Signposts of certainty
Set to remind us,
Grey is the washed-out
Approach of the dawning…
   We lay in the caravan,
   Made love till morning.

We sat at the seafront
To watch the grey rollers
We saw careworn mothers
Behind their grey strollers,
Such is the love that
These lives have been born in…
   To lie in a caravan
   Make love till morning…

10 September 1973

Mittagong

I drove you through the mistlands
At sleepy Mittagong,
My car was like a stately coach
With its minions overcome,
The road was like a ribbon of light
A-twist in a fairy dell,
But lost in front, and lost behind
As we entered the fairy spell.

The trees rose out of the sylvan scene
Like a giant mushroom glade,
And silver dripped from our wondering eyes
As we saw the land they played.
I laid your head in disbelief
On a silken cushion, fairly,
For this was seen at Mittagong
At five in the morning early.

17 September 1973

Romany Girl

Romany girl on the silver sand
What would you have me yearning,
To take you into my loving arms
While the world lay waste, and burning
To touch the sheen of your auburn hair
While the stars look on in wonder,
And watch the hem of your gypsy dress
That tears my heart asunder.

Romany girl, is your lovely name
The Jean of a witch returning,
Or just the touch of a love-lost fool
Who's seeking your brown eyes burning,
The spell of lace at your pretty face
Or caught at your throat a-bunching,
Or sweetness smile of your guiltless guile
Bewitching the Squire, a-lunching.

Romany girl, who struts and sways
To dance at the morning graces,
Setting the sand in either hand
To laugh at the wondering faces,
Images burn the fevered brain
Of a man who's never been tipsy,
Dance on the silver sand again
And look for your love-lost gypsy.

18 September 1973

Dark Forces

There's something a-move in your mind, girl,
Some deepest dark danger to you,
There's something apace in the cloud and your grace
So intent on bewildering you.

There's something in moon-shadowed buildings and barns
And your eyes in the eventime dusk,
And the shiver of nothingness sweeping the hedgerows
Of moon-glaring pillars of rust.

There's something in forces and tides of the night
That is sweeping the eyes of your mind,
And pools of translucent, emotional movement
Envelope the well of your kind.

There's something that dwells in the well of your kind
That retreats in a whisper from light,
But always tick-ticks at the moment the sun sinks
To drown in the sea of the night.

10 October 1973

The Old Grey Man of the Sea

Sat at the edge of a rickety boat that is
Stranded in time and in tide,
Caught in the mists of the visions you see
In the cloud on the seaward side,
What do you dream of the stories of old,
And what was the memory;
The coastal cottagers spreading their nets...
Or the old, grey man of the sea?

Whenever the weather is humid and close and the
Cloud sits heavy on me,
I look at the picture of you and the boat
And the cloud and the sand and the sea,
I see in your face all the memories held,
The memories held from me,
Of the coastal cottagers spreading their nets
And the old grey man of the sea.

25 November 1973

When the Gypsy Crystal Fell

Jeannie, what have you done to me
In the mystery of your smile,
Have you caught my soul in a tangled dream
To twist my web awhile,
Have you fashioned one of your gypsy charms
To lock my heart in your lovely arms
Or caught my mind in your spell,
As the gypsy crystal fell?

Jeannie, where is the twist of fate
That set me on my heels,
Did I catch a ride on a Jeannie tide
To see how a captive feels,
Was I whisked away on a Summer's day
To find you waiting a world away
A-dream of a gypsy dell,
In the spell of a wishing well?

Jeannie, why do you sigh and say
That a man is only a man,
But a witch's dreams and a gypsy's schemes
Are harder to understand,
Did I see at night the enchanted sight
Of the Jean I've seen in the candlelight
While drifting under your spell,
As the gypsy crystal fell?

25 November 1973

Love-Lost

When the first sweet burst of love and lust
Has eddied and ebbed to dreams and dust,
Has eddied and ebbed in the tide of my head
To the essence of dreams and dust;

And once the passionate nights are spent
In sipping the wine the gods repent,
In sipping the wine that's tipping my mind
To find that my mind is spent;

And when the smile that you have for me
Has slipped and dipped for eternity,
Has slipped and dipped in the wayward shift
Of the love that you have for me;

I think I'll sit and I'll sigh at night
To drift and dream to the dawning light,
To drift and dream in the dreams and dust
That I hold of you in the candlelight.

20 November 1973

Larkspur

Words roll free from a tongue sometime
From a sometime, tongue-tied tongue,
Words that were heard by the stream and the bird
When the world and the wild were young,
When the world and the wild were young, sometime…
    (Larkspur, marigold, ebony, lime).

Sounds that were born in sweet young breath
In a bubble-sighed, trouble-tried time,
Sounds that were found by a child at the breast
In a bubble-tried pantomime,
In a bubble-tried pantomime, no less…
    (Nightshade, cinnamon, green watercress).

Love is the sound of a word, soft-said
From the lips of the love you too,
Love is the dove of the bubble-thought read
Soft sift from the me to you,
Soft sift from the me to you, soft said…
    (Homespun, empathy, marmalade, bread).

16 December 1973

-1974-

Another Moment More

I've run out of tales for the telling,
I've run out of points of view,
I've run out of time for the nursery rhyme
Whose moral is left to you,
I've never been high on pie in the sky
And now that I've lost that too,
I've run out of legs for the running,
From what, and whatever, to who.

When you're worn and you're tired, and ugly,
And you're living from day to day,
You're torn by the things that you should have done,
And the things that you ought to say,
You think of the chances lost to you
Whenever you turned your head,
Then wait for the chance to arise again,
To lose another instead.

So if I should say 'I love you',
In a breathless moment past,
As I'm rushing out through the open door
To take that chance, at last,
Forgive the times that I turned my head
To lose the chance before,
And love me too with your open arms
For another moment more!

31 January 1974

Water or Milk

All I can offer you;
Water or milk,
Dreams for your lonely ones,
Sadness and silk,
Schemes for your dreamers and
Thread for your seamers to
Weave in a tapestry
Of some other ilk.

All that I ask of you
Eyes for your sight,
Ears for your listening to
Sounds in the night.
Cheers for the lucky ones, hear-
Hears for the plucky ones and
Tears for the loved ones who
Dropped out of sight.

1 March 1974

Three Starlings

I've seen three starlings in the sun-set
And the cold wind blows all over,
Three starlings flown from the Russian Front
Til the cold wind blow blows over.

Til the cold war wind blows over all
In the cold of the cold war warring,
Three starlings sit in the English mist
With the English Channel calling.

16 March 1974

Sweetness and Light

Anything's possible, Sweetness and Light,
Maybe you'll leave me lonely,
Maybe you'll stir like a shade in the night
To turn to your one and only.
On a fine morning you'll probably say
'I've looked at you once too often…'
And I'll look in vain for the signs and the tides
Of your looks and your voice to soften.

Anything's possible, Sweetness and Light
Maybe you'll leave me never,
Maybe I'll grow in your mind and your sight
'Til I fill your horizons forever!
On a fine evening you'll possibly say:
'You know that I've followed your star!'
And I in my turn will take Sweetness and Light
To the Sweetness and Light that you are.

26 March 1974

Cast No Dark Shadows

Cast no dark shadows,
Leave me enlightened,
Watch for my darkness and
Hold me when frightened,
Let your love follow me
Along to my fall;
Keep no false secrets but
Tel me them all.

Say all you have to say,
Leave naught unsaid,
One morning early you
May find me dead,
I need your everything to
Take in my mind,
Give of your loveliness and
All that you find.

Let there be nothing left
Unsaid when you find me,
God, how I love you and
Need you behind me,
Let me take loneliness
Away from your grief;
Cast no dark shadows, and
I'll be your thief.

17 May 1974

Stand Up & Be Counted

In the days of our beginnings when this
love was bitter born, and the infamies of lovers
was the subject of their scorn,
when the people slandered children in the
cheapness of their lives, and a man was ever
martyred to the spite of bitter wives,
we would swallow disillusion for the sake of
hanging on, to the beauty or the passion or
the love that we had known,

we would hold ourselves erect to brave the
bitterness again, for the folly and the anger
and the spite of bitter men.

But I held you in the country as you
faltered and you fell, in the volleys of the cynics
and our private little hell,
so we hid ourselves from everything the
world could say in spite, and I watched you
suffer slowly in the emptiness of night,
but we found it getting harder by the day to
sit and smile, for the sickness of the people
cuts and runs a ragged mile,
and the sickness of the people has the taste
of bitter bread, when you're vilified and
ostracised and wish that you were dead.

If they only knew that marriage has a
steady course to run, and that once that
course is over then the marriage is undone,
and that no amount of vehemence can
make a marriage last, if the love is left a
dusty memory of pleasures past,
or if once a bond thus torn apart can leave
the couple free to find happiness with others,
that's the way it ought to be,
but the sickness of the people is that
marriage always clings, feeds its bitterness
and heartache in the hopelessness it brings.

So we came back to the city, and we
came back to the scorn, and we often cursed
our mothers for the day that we were born,
but we carried on in silence and denied

that we were wrong, we were lovers with a
vengeance, we were right and we were strong,
though I often felt you moving in the dark
to cry aloud at the vicious dream attacks,
and at the banter of the crowd,
but you very rarely murmured of your many
sleepless nights, and I told you very little
of my own disturbing sights.

It was all so long ago that they can each forget
the pain that they inflicted on the lovers, though
the burning scars remain,
and to tell them would do nothing but
arouse their instant ire, till they taste their
bitter acid, or their testing in the fire,
for the choice will come to many; do we
stay in misery, do we separate to love again
and, are we really free,
can we stand the vicious malice of the
people's twisted grace, or stay miserable and
shatter every mirror in the place.

25 May 1974

Deadpan

What will you do now, Peter Brown,
Where will this madness end?
Will you ride your knight to the castle light
To sight your loveless friend?
Will you take your Queen to the village green
Where all the vows were sworn,
Or slip away like a piece in play
To act as the bishop's pawn?

What will the end be, Peter Brown,
Now that your King's in check?
Will you slip a pawn to a surly Queen
To save your coward's neck?
Will you fortify 'til the bishop's men
Call checkmate to your steed,
Or lead the play in your careless way
And lose the piece you need?

9 July 1974

The Telegram

Darling girl, will you love me now
That I've left you far behind me,
I took the plane in the driving rain
And I doubt that you could find me,
I left the part of my heart behind
That all my love was laid in,
And found that all of my life with you
Was the part I should have stayed in.

Mistress mine, will you miss the touch
Of a man whose miss is touching
The silken skin of a mistress sin
Whose sin was trust in trusting.
Be still, be sure of your faith in one
Who knows your own sweet sorrow,
And watch for me in the sky tonight
For I may be home tomorrow.

9 July 1974

The Mother of My Life

So you told your closest friends that you're
The mother of my life, that you've made the
Great decision, (though you're not my lawful wife),
And I heard in saddened silence how your heart
(Behind the words), beat a rapid hesitation as
Your resolution stirred.
But you smiled and chattered gaily in the
Innocence of play, as my throat refused to
Yield a single word I thought to say;

Will you love this life,
Be my lover, be my wife,
Will you say again tomorrow
You're the mother of my life?

For my seed is deep within you at the
Stirring of the dawn, will you hold my seed
Within you 'til the day our child is born?
Will you cherish, (as you say you cherished

Love that put it there), will it perish in your
Hesitation, lost beyond a care?
Will you make a firm decision, be it aye
Or be it nay, in the shades of Caesar's Legions
Let this gladiator say;

As you love this land,
Love this life, this heart and hand,
Will you scatter forth the seed
Or be the mother of a man?

28 July 1974

Musicmaker

I see black moods of cloudy thought
Flung out on some strange shifting tide,
I feel some moving spirit stir and
Catch my mind and breath, the bride
Of depth and wisdom, long denied.

And when I cast spasmodic lines
From pen and ink in helpless grace
I sit bemused, a fortune's fool who
Knows not where the drift, the lace
Of nature's framework shows her face.

But you immerse your mind in frets
And keys and chords, and silken strings
To mould my fumbled, clumsy thought
Within melodic scores, the things
I only felt, within you sings.

And I've sat in some corner shade
While you poured out my shifting tide,
The words a spirit stirred in me
Fell silently away, to glide
Toward some distant shore, I cried.

3 August 1974

Heath - (b. 2 August 1974 d.)

I've sat and I've wondered for night after night
In the dim, dying glow of the flame,
While the silence has settled in wave upon wave
On the bitterness burnt in my brain,
How fickle the fortune of man in his dreams,
How senseless the twist of his fate,
We cry in the way of the quick and the lost
But our cries and our tears are too late!

My son, had he lived, would have been such a man
As the earth, in its need, smiled upon,
Who would conquer the ladies, the killers of men
Where the moon or the bright sun shone,
Who'd aspire to the heights in the life that he lived,
Both loved and respected by all,
Who would smile upon me as his father, and hold
A young arm out to steady my fall.

And some afternoons in the twilight of life
As the autumns slipped out in the cold,
We would sit, and we'd laugh, and we'd jolly the part
In remembered forgottens of old,

While his sweet, pretty wife would bring cartons of ice
When the afternoon sun grew apace,
And smile at the son she had borne to my son
In her joy, and blue wrappings of lace.

Tell me, my son, if you'd lived would it be
As I've said, would you comfort my tears?
Would you look at your mother, who loved all your life
As her own, would you settle her fears?
Oh my son, when you slipped so impossibly far
From this life on that warm August night,
I cried for the loss of your love and your presence,
You birth, and your death, and your light!

28 August 1974

Lost August

'Oh, it's not that I want to be awkward,'
She began, as he stifled a sigh,
'Though I don't understand your intentions,
And I'm not even going to try…'
'I will bow to your final decision,' he said,
In this, as in all we have done,
Only, please try to show me some kindness
As the man you once loved for your own.'

She looked from the living room window
Her arms tightly crossed at the breast,
Her back was so sternly toward him
That he feared for the worst, (and the best),

'There once was a time,' then she halted,
Some things were left better unsaid,
Then she sighed, 'Well, it's just for one Christmas...
Then she snarled, 'But I wish you were dead.'

And he smiled, as she turned back to face him
In that wistful expression of old,
Where his mouth turned the corners up lightly
But his eyes cried their hurt in the cold.
'Yes, it's only for Christmas I'm asking
With our children again at the last,
I'll be gone with the wind in the morning,
Just a memory drift in your past.'

Then he felt that he should have said something
So he muttered: 'I'm sorry… and that',
And he turned down his gaze to the carpet,
And he felt for his old, beaten hat.
'Don't go… would you care for a coffee…'
She haltingly started to say,
As he fumbled his hat in confusion
To nod his familiar way.

'If you'd rather I went,' he said quickly,
'I know this is painful for you….'
'Don't be soft,' said his wife from the kitchen,
'It's long since I felt owt for you…'
'If you'd only been more of a husband,
Or more of a father to them…'
'Yes, I know,' and he painfully nodded,
And stared at the carpet again.

'Well, you'll sleep on the floor, in the study,
And I don't want you wandering round,
I've a man, as you know, that I sleep with,

And I won't have him feeling put down.'
Then the hurt of his glance must have touched her,
'Well, I'm sorry, but that's how it is,
Either sleep in the study...' he nodded,
And accepted with grace his defeat.

'As a matter of interest', she started,
As she carried the tray through the door,
'Where on earth did you go... back in August
(He just smiled at some point on the floor).
'Was it some fancy woman you wanted
While I spent the nights sitting alone,
Spent the days in a panic, and staring
In the hopes that you'd write, or you'd phone?'

'I'm sorry,' he muttered, 'I'm sorry,
I know it was terribly wrong...
As he sat huddled up in the corner,
(And he'd once been so straight and so strong),
So strong and so young and romantic,
So faithful as well... she appeared
Once again in the line of his vision
With the slightest veiled hint of a sneer.

'I'll be off then, I'll see you on Sunday,'
Then he rushed through the door and was gone
And the tears welled again at her eyelids
As she felt so adrift and alone.
'What is done has been done and forgotten,
I'm soft for the beggar, I know.'
Then the children rushed in at the doorway...
'Was that Daddy we saw up the road?'

On the night before Christmas, a shadow
Slid wearily up to the door,

And the head was both bowed and defeated,
And the coat was both ragged and torn,
But she hid the distaste as she took it
And noticed how aged he'd become,
As he went to the study in silence,
And she went to her bed with her man.

He emerged at the break of the dawning
Midst the cries of delight at the tree,
And he basked in their love and attention
As he balanced them both on his knee.
But his wife was a trifle distracted
For her man wouldn't come, at the last,
'I'll be gone with the wind...' he repeated,
'Just a memory drift in your past.'

And he'd gone as he'd promised, when morning
Saw all the festivities done,
With the love and regrets of his children
And a last, loving kiss for his son...
'Yes it's only for Christmas I'm asking
With our children again at the last,'
He was gone with the wind in the morning,
Just a memory drift in her past.

But the New Year was carelessly breaking
And the memories slipping away
When the police brought the news in the morning
That he'd died on the previous day.
'Do you mean that he'd kept it a secret,
I'll be damned,' said the Sergeant again,
'He knew he was riddled with cancer,
What a man, what a man among men!'

So she cried… but it wasn't in anger,
Just the soft, helpless cry of defeat...
Did he think it would be any better,
Did he think he could temper her grief?
'As a matter of interest,' she'd started
As she'd carried the tray through the door,
'Where on earth did you go, back in August...
He'd just smiled at a point on the floor.

Now whenever she passes her lover
They both turn their faces away,
He went back to his job in munitions
And his wife, it was better that way...
If he'd only been more of a husband,
Or more of a father, she'd said,
And she'd sighed, 'Well it's just for one Christmas...'
And she'd snarled, 'But I wish you were dead!'

And he'd smiled as she'd turned back to face him
In that wistful expression of old,
Where his mouth turned the corners up lightly
But his eyes cried their hurt in the cold.
'Yes, it's only for Christmas I'm asking,
With our children again, at the last,
I'll be gone with the wind in the morning,
Just a memory drift in your past.'

21 September, 1974

Jane O'Grady

Grey old lady, sat by the sea
With her nimble fingers, weaving,
Jane O'Grady, seventy three
In the world that she was leaving.
Hummed sweet honey from virgin lips
In the way of the wind, sad-sighing,
Carried the song from her fingertips
To the day that she lay dying.

Shuttle sang in the early breeze
To the tune of life's sweet sorrow:
"God, I'm weary of weaving love,
But I'll not be here tomorrow."

Grey old lady, worked with a will
On the shawl of life's sweet pattern,
Fingers stilled in the dawning chill
As the world turned once too often!
Nevermore will she weave the love
That we borrowed, all unknowing,
Only the rags of the hand-me-downs
With the grey wind blowing.

24 November 1974

Further Down the Line

'It's better for some than for others
In the sway and the way of the world,
For there's never a cut and dried answer,
To your cut and dried questions, my girl.
Yes, I know that it's hard on assistance
Since everyone went to the wall,
I've stood in the line since September,
And I'll stand 'til the government falls.'

'I've seen children stand for their fathers
In the line, for an hour or more,
With the lines by the week getting longer
As we file through the government's door,
And the faces I've seen hold no visions
Of Europe, or travel abroad,
Just a face-saving job in a warehouse,
Just a job - that's the only reward!'

'Is he mad', said the girl in reflection,
'Can't he see us all here on the dole?
Has he ever stood deep in a two hour queue,
Does he care, does the man have a soul?
When the people have need of a leader....'
But the end of the line was near;
I wished her a most Merry Christmas,
And a prosperous, Happy New Year!'

16 December 1974

Christmas 1974

I've heard all the scratched plastic carols
In stereo, five ninety-five,
I've paid my John Martin's admission
To help keep the season alive,
I've done all I could for the children
To keep Father Christmas in beer,
I've scrimped and I've saved my emotion
To see out the last of the year.

I don't take my cheer in a bottle,
My marriage has gone to the wall,
The kids are away with their mother
There isn't a shot left to call,
There's a tree that is tinselled and winking
With no-one to see on the day,
I'm keeping their presents 'til later
To think of them, while they're away.

So if this is the great celebration
The spirit in me passed away,
And I haven't the spirit to mourn it,
Its passing, its death or decay.
I'll go to the church about midnight
To pray, with a thought from the heart,
For Christ, it's your Mass we're fulfilling
Before we start falling apart.

19 December 1974

One Step On

I can see the pit of darkness stretched
Before my hapless eyes
And another week should see me in its fold,
For my steps have long been faster
At the brink of my disaster
When the master plan refuses to be told.

But from some deep, hidden augury,
Eternal stories spring,
And the loss of me may be some other's gain,
If it weren't for bitter memories
Dredged from the darkening rill
Of your being, I might even love again.

I remember how the forays first
Were thwarted at the pass,
Where your armies dug in tight around your eyes,
How my heavy armour failed me
And your cynicism railed,
But a flower brought the first of your replies.

And from some embattled ridge
I first saw the silver bridge
Of your smile, though it settled not on me.
Till my squad of engineers, filled your
Eyes and mouth and ears,
With the sight and taste and sound of certainty.

And a frontal, forced attack, sent you
Reeling, wheeling back,
With my armour at the gates of your defence,

So I strutted through the posterns of
Your dilettantish mind,
And the masque of each and every sad pretence.

But my victory was over long
Before I lost the war
In the clinging mire of Flander's muddy gown,
And I tried to pull my army back
From Dunkirk's smooth and silken rack,
But floundered in the rigor of your frown.

My armies have been scattered and
I'm chained at the abyss
Of your tempers, and the emptiness of mine,
Though your love is all-consuming at
The height of your desire,
Your frantic freedoms warn you to decline.

I'm afraid of hidden mists and things
Unknown that may persist
When in the future gloom I'm cast without a light,
For my army has been battered, beaten,
Broken up and scattered, leaving
No intrigues to see me through the night.

In the furnace of your brain my
Burning image will remain,
Despite your search to quench your mad desire,
Though I'm lost to all I knew, I'll be
Better off than you,
For darkness burns a cooler flame than fire.

25 February 1975

One Word Swallowed

Ah!… Ah!… What is Man?
The sad slick-sliver of the long quicksand,
The flash-burst crackle of the lightning, forking
Or two young daughters of the evening, talking.

Lord!… Lord!… What is pain?
The short sharp splinters of the mad March rain,
The last lost touch of any man's need, needing
Or one word swallowed as the other word's leaving.

Girl!… Girl!… What is love?
The daydream dreaming at the first faint flush,
The cool kiss sipping at the breath, fresh-tasting
Or black sheets buried in your bared limbs, waiting?

28 February 1975

Ashes & Dust

I've been for a stroll by the midnight beach
That I've waited to stroll so long for,
I've taken a look at the lover's breach
That a fellow I knew wrote a song for,
The sea is as calm as a mid-summer balm
At the welcoming cool of the dawning,
I've a woman in bed who has sleep in her head
That I'll never get up in the morning.

It's never the same when you come back again
To relive the old passions remembered,
The fires have almost gone out, as they must,
And all you are left with are ashes and dust.

There once was a time when a night would be spent
In a lust that your body believed in,
A frantic few hours of parry and thrust
With a woman who wasn't deceiving,
The day must be dead; she's a spring in her head
That is wound to the point of breaking,
But all I can see is the sleep and the sea
And the love that we ought to be making.

It's never the same when you come back again
To relive the old passions expended,
All of your thoughts and your hopes, as they must,
Are left with your memories, ashes and dust.

1 March 1975

In a Cemetery…

Islands of memories
Cities of stone,
Sentinels of silence
In the great all-alone,
'What do you find in
Your new-found release?'
Sigh-whispered silence, girl:
'Peace, perfect peace!'

Youth fresh from aging,
Love's bloom anew,
Old friends re-greeting
The girl they once knew,
Those who have loved you
In life's livid crease
Hold to your memory in
Peace, perfect peace!

11 March, 1975

Tallyn Tor

'I'm only the flotsam, jetsam drift
Cast up on your bars and beaches,
The glittering shift that you can't resist
When viewed from your northern reaches,
I didn't come down in a thunderstorm
Or a blast from your heaven's lightning,
But cast ashore from the devil's maw
As the jaws of the storm were tightening.'

'You watched from the walls of Tallyn Tor
My stars and clouds surround me,
The smoke and drift of an ancient shift
That will always whirlwind round me.
Not even the peace of a lonely beach
Could trouble the storm that caught me
For I sink or swim in the storm within,
Not the eye of the storm that brought me!'

'Deep in the halls of Tallyn Tor
Your hand was the hand to greet me,
And during the wintering months of war
Did your fevered storms defeat me.
If ever the tide should turn, should turn
In claiming its own around it,
I'll leave the beach and the lover's reach
As empty as flotsam found it.'

14 March 1975

The Old Wife's Mood

'Don't grumble and growl and roar at me
Old man, when your temper's turning,
I've long since tired of your vain disputes
In the halls of your lordship's learning,
You think, old man, you can tame me now
By beating your breakers shoreward,
I've never put up with your antics yet
When your spume is fuming forward!'

'Don't shriek at me,' said the old man sea
As she whipped at his crests in temper,
'It's always the way that your humour turns
Each bleak and harsh September;
Will ever you calm yourself, you witch
And settle my troubled rancour,
Or shriek and howl like a grey old owl
At my spindrift's sullen anger?'

'Old, I was old when the world was young
In my hallowed depths and deeps,
What did I want with a wife like you
Whose temper never sleeps?'
'Don't carp and cavil at me,' she shrilled
In the runnels at rocks uncovered,
'I'd turn the tide in a backward slide
For the sake of a new-found lover.'

She turned to whip at the whining wires:
'I'm leaving you and your brood,'
The sea came grumbling round the Pier
'It's only the old wife's mood!
She's light and happy in other months,
In love that's ever the way...'
The old wife crept from her hiding place
To join him, out in the bay.

15 March 1975

Déjà vu

'What have you done to your head again?'

'The sea flowed out and the wind blew in
To the purple mist at the Do-drop Inn
As I went to say what I said I'd seen....'
'Surely you said,
       you said...'

'If all your thought, like a Comet's burst
Was a witches damn, or a tinker's curse
While a sailor's caul made the ship reverse

Whenever he turned his head...'
    'you said...'

'Shallow and sorry, the same response
Of the one who never to one belongs
And never to more than one the once,
Guarding the maidenhead...'
    'you said...'

'It's hard, so hard to arrange the mind
In the tints and colours of humankind
When the reds are Red, and the blind are blind
To everything surely said...'
    'you said...'

'I went to say what I said I'd seen
In the purple mist at the Do-drop Inn
As the sea flowed out and the wind blew in...'

'What have you done to your head again?'

9 May 1975

The Wizard of Clayton Close

He's steeped in the shadows of ivy and stone,
And time is the seed that the Wizard has sown,
Has sown for the magick of weaving the night
In a tapestry taken from burning delight.
Burning delight in the eyes of the mind he has
Stolen, to conjure insight for the blind, for the
Blind are the pebbles that litter his beach, while the
Tides of his mind set the blind out of reach.

The masonry wall is caught deep in the spell that he
Conjured forgotten, in some distant dell,
And if you should peer through the ivy and stone
There's a voice whispers... 'leave me, just leave me alone.
I've wandered with Ishtar, away from your eyes
From your spying and prying, away from your lies,
In the peril and terror that lonely men speak...
Seek not the undying, whatever you seek.'

But drawn to the shadows and drawn to the stone
I could leave him not ever, not leave him alone,
And turning one day to the light and the lace
He uncovered his forehead, uncovered his face.
I froze in the instant to question my mind for
The face spoke eternities, infinite time
And the stars held their place in the lips of the man
And the cheeks and the ears, and the eyes and the hand.

The wall crumbled inward as slowly I fell
Through his eyes to the stars, to the depths of his well,
And knowledge was mine as it never had been,
In my mind, misaligned, in the things that I'd seen.
But knowledge was danger, disaster and death
To the heart that would beat, to the mind, to the breath,
To the cheek of a girl or the smile of a man,
To the whisp' of the wind, to the shift of the sand.

And nothing exists in the nothing of me
But the stars and the sky, and the sand and the sea,
The light that was night and the dark of the day
As I drift in the tides of his vision away.
And look as I might for the eyes of his mind

I believe that the Wizard is totally blind,
That once in the depths of his well and his breath
We're imprisoned in freedom, the freedom from death.

If only the way was as clearly defined
In the world of the deaf and the dumb and the blind,
I'd crawl through the stars to the lids of his eyes
To the breadth of his world and the width of his lies.
For the comfort of woman and warmth of a man
I would give all the shift and the sift of the sand,
And not all the shadows of ivy and stone
Would lure me to walk in the winter alone.

21 May 1975

Why Do We Write?

'I thought you would learn by this,
I gave you more than your due,
You scribblers waste your pen and ink
For a readership, so few!
But you learn less than most,
For you refuse to learn,
That the cause is lost when you count the cost
As you watch your papers burn!'

'And what do the people care
For the things you shout about?
Do you think there's one gives a tinker's cuss
For your place on the roundabout?

You can't get through to the Church,
You can't shout up to the steeple,
And if you climb up to the bats and bells
You can't be heard by the people!'

I looked at the man once more,
At the jeering mouth and eye:
'What would you know of the heart that beats
At the soul of the midnight cry?
I'll write for the man that reads,
I'll shout from the Church and steeple,
Should the voice or the word be never heard
I'm still with the living people!'

6 June 1975

Now That I'm Mad!

Why don't you visit me,
Why be so sad,
Twilight is wizardry
Now that I'm mad;
Moonbeams are paper chains
Drifting in lovers lanes
Life, merely labour pains
Or some passing fad.

Why don't you visit me
Is it for shame?
What is in sanity
That sullies your name?
I'd rather seek delight
In some distant candle-light

Than worry the wanton night
At life's cruel game!

10 June 1975

The Star

When I was a boy I searched the skies
For the truth, a star, and the worldly wise,
But ever the path of the brightest lay
On my neighbour's roof, or another's way.

So I chose a star and I called it 'Dawn'
As the brightest light in a summer storm
And I charged it: 'Lay out my future way
As bright as the path you trace today.'

But when I was older, learned and wise
I left the star in the drifting skies
And never a thought of the star was lent
While the truth, the star, and my faith was spent.

And when I was down, and worn, and thin,
I got to think what I might have been
And searched for the star in the drifting skies
And cried its name at the pale sunrise.

I've scanned and searched for a single star
Since the way of the world was far too far,
But all I get are the skies alight
Or a deep despair on a cloudy night!

5 July 1975

The Last Trump

I seem to recollect a certain
Glass wheel, dreaming,
Spinning in the face of those who fell,
Whose mute misunderstanding was
The sum of those left standing
As the gaoler let the prisoners from the cell.

And God was on the balcony
With nothing left to do
But to let the ledgers settle in the dust,
Accounts they brought before him,
Totals carried, balanced for him
Settled nothing but a patent lack of trust.

But the eyes on the horizon where
The sea swept into space
Caught some troubled gaze of mine
And shed a star,
'If there's any wish within you
Make it now, before the tide
Of my dying sweeps you further than you are.'

Then I woke and found the letter that
You'd left me once before
When we'd slipped from love and
Lost each other's grace,
And I cried into the morning at
The tail-lights of your car:
'God above, don't ever let me lose your face!'

23 July 1975

The Morning Sun

The first dawn breaks
The morning sun
Glows redly in
The hearts of men,
And morning light
With shadows soft
Gives hope and cheer
To every man!

At noon, in toil
And sweat he stands
To serve the dreams
Within his bounds,
But rarely sees
The roving sun
Move on toward
The afternoon.

For when harsh shadows
Break the ground
He toiled and tilled
When he was sound,
The memories of
The morning sun
Come back to haunt him,
Every one!

And thus he lives
In some dim dream
Unknowing how
To set him free,

But weaves the patterns
Of the sun...
Conceived in mutual misery.

6 September 1975

Toll Not My Bell

For some is death
A distant dream
Like riders warring,
Grim and bleak,
While others fear
Its stealthy tread
Or whispered breath
On withered cheek.

And some are torn
And some lie still
To cling to warmth
In love's embrace,
And some are born
To hold the tapered
Candle to
Another's grace.

Who rolls the dice
To score the card,
Who spins the orbs
In endless space?
What hand will set
The border bounds
Of planets in
Some poet's face?

And once my sand
Has trickled low
With weary lines
That others spend,
God grant the strength
To leave some thought
From such of life
I've never penned.

6 September 1975

Into the Light

- I -

Here I am, twenty-one,
So many things have to be done,
Many's the cause I'll be fighting for
Keeping the vows that I've sworn before,
How many children blessing my way,
How much love can a lover sway,
How many words can I write and read
In the years ahead for my restless need,
Where am I headed, this fateful night…
*Out of the darkness
Into the light!*

- II -

Here I am, thirty-one,
So many things still to be done;

Where are the causes? Fought and lost!
What of the vows? Tempest tossed!
Where are the children? Left behind!
What of the lovers? Love is blind!
How many words have you written and read?
Much too much for this aching head.
Where are you headed, this fateful night?
    Out of the darkness
    Into the light!

- III -

Here I am, forty-one,
And all life seems like a dream undone.
Everything I would have taken for me
Has slipped from my grasp, forsaken me.
All my children are grown, but one
And wonder; 'Where did this man come from?
What was the pact that he kept with me…'
While I have nothing to answer thee!
All my words as a mist, widespread
Have since dispersed from a source long dead.
Where am I headed, this fateful night?
    (Have you learned nothing….?)
    I guess you're right!

- IV -

Here I am, fifty-one,
The daylight fades and the muse has gone.
The loves I loved as my vision bled
All turned from me, and to them, I'm dead.
The rhyme was lost and the music died

As I turned to stone in my heart, inside.
Where is the youth that yearned to write
Through the endless days to the latest night?
Is this what happens, the years take flight –
> *Into the darkness*
> *Out of the light.*

- V -

Here I am, sixty-one,
I thought the end would have come and gone!
But then a light seemed to beckon me
To trip through another's history.
When China called, I know not why
I saw new future's I'd never tried,
The way was clear, my life was spent
So I fetched up in the Orient.
With all its bustle, its pomp, and pride,
I picked up the pen that I'd put aside,
For black-haired girls feed my heart's content
And children like jewels are heaven sent;
Is this the future, I know it's right....
> Out of the darkness
> Into the light.

I & II - 22 November 1975
III -   16 June 1986
IV -   20 March 1996
V -   26 December 2005

If You Die

If you die, I shall smash all the windows,
And I'll burn all the pictures of you,
I shall kick down the doors
And I'll tear up the floors
If you die...
If you dare...
If you do!
And you'll never be safe in the hurt and the hate
Though you lie and stare sightlessly back,
For I'll batter your face to destroy any grace
You've preserved...
                For the life that you lack!

Then I'll claw at your arms and your fingers
So they'll never hold anyone new,
And I'll mark both your thighs
In the light of your lies
If you die...
If you dare...
If you do!
I will scream in your ears 'til your eyes fill with tears
In remorse for the love we once knew,
And I'll bite at your lips and your dead fingertips
So the pain
           Of the living comes through.

If you die, I shall wander at midnight
Through the darkest of forest and fen,

I shall cry out your shame
As the wind takes your name
If you die...
      If you leave me again!

8 December 1975

Who Cares?

What ever happens when a love goes wrong
When a love goes wrong some morning,
Goes wrong like the singer of a blackbird song
That a blackbird's not been born in?
Lost like the flutter of a butterfly's flight
In the wild south wind's clash-clatter,
Or a heartbeat stopped as an oak tree's lopped;
Who cares?
Why? What does it matter?

What ever happens to a love-lost love
To a love-lost love, come Autumn,
Or a bare beech, birch, or a grey stone church
Or the leaves that the birch tree brought them;
To walk in the shelter of a shaded lane
With the last of the lost love's chatter,
Like the half of a whole, or a lonely soul,
Who cares?
Why? What does it matter?

What ever happens to the other one - you
To the other you, half a love lonely,
Do you care, do you weep, do you rest, do you sleep
When you love alone, loving me only?

Will you heave some sigh in your memory's eye
For the scenes of our springtime laughter,
Or burn some flame to erase my name...
Who cares?
Why? What does it matter?

11 December 1975

-1976-

The Last Word

And so to this then,
The last word on the last word penned.
The tides of life have caught me unaware,
And in the depths and shallows
I have found my heart's despair.
Buoyed on the breakers
Floundering in the troughs,
A sense of life and love was all
I ever really lost.
Surging at the floodtide,
Clawing at the rip,
I foundered on your reef
Like some old, grey ship.

But now as you lie
In your straight, narrow bed
Made three years long
By this self-same head,

My heart lies wrecked
On my own home shore...
If I'd loved you less
You'd have loved me more.
If the then was the now
As it was, once more,
I would seal my lips
As I've done before,
I'd release my mind
From this butcher's hook...
And I'd tear every page
From your colouring book.

31 January 1976

The Dog 'Sat' on the Tucker Box...

As I was driving slowly by
Some Gundagai or other, I
Was heard to sigh, or make remark
'The Tucker Dog has lost his bark –
His bite as well, (or so they tell),
Which probably is just as well
And other nasty habits which
Are said to ruin sandwiches!'

If I were known as Bullock Jack
And some dog on my tucker 'sat',
I'd not be raising marble slabs
But rather hell, the roof, red rags.
And when that dog had done his bit,
(That word, I dare not mention it),

I'd ram that sandwich where no rabbit
Ever crawled, to cure the habit!

31 January 1976

Losing You

If, in the end
There's just a waste of days,
With naught to please
For all those words of praise,
And none to share the memories
That we knew.....
Then I'll have lost my all
              In losing you...

1 February 1976

English Tides

I'm trapped within my past of English days,
Of English sights and sounds, and English ways,
For though some stranger took me at the flood
I still feel drums of England in my blood.

And though these eighteen years have seen the swell
Of foreign ports and strands command my spell,
Within these veins run many a peasant stream
Of English woods, of English tides and dreams.

18 April 1976

In Regret

I've heard your most familiar voice
A million times, my friend,
But why does friendship lead us on
To nothing, in the end?
We clasp the hand, and smile and say:
'I'll see you in the spring,
When fate is shifting shadows
On the stage and in the wings.'
When fate is shifting shadows,
We perceive but cannot see...
What shadows crossed our stage that night
To kill the friend in me?

I've listened to the music that
You conjured in some dream,
The better half of words that came
Half-formed in all I've seen,
The better half of all you would
Aspire to do, or be,
Your music woke the better half
Of words I found in me.
Your music woke the better half
Of friendship, long ago
O how I wish that I could see
You make that music now.

The light that burns the candle
Always sputters at the end,
The light we burned was bright, too bright
For you and I, my friend!
The season closed its shutters
And the winters came in swift

For I lost sight of your manner,
Of your mind and of its drift;
And I think you lost the essence of
The flesh that makes my kind
When you took me for some stranger
With a pen and paper mind!

14 July 1976

Short Shrift

I've failed!' How many times have sons
And fathers' fathers echoed me?
'I've failed! My life was spent in dreams,'
We said, 'in shallow misery.
In dreams and steel and soot and grime,
In screams, and what would seem some crime
Of trying to live beyond our need...
Our lives were spent in some black creed!'

'Too short, too short, the days we spent
In trying to right the days before,
Too long, too long, the years we struggled
Knowing not what struggled for.
What goal, what aim, what discontent,
What loves we lost, what life we spent
In wondering what such life could be?
Short shrift for you - harsh words for me!'

'I've failed, my sons, I've failed you all
And so my failure tortures me,
As in that innocence divine

Your love loves all the failed in me.
If I could strip this flesh, or tear
These eyes that cried hot fire for you
To save you from the same despair
My father's father brought me to...'

20 July 1976

Looking Back (1963-76)

I've often thought that all the time
We spent, in spending wasted all,
And lost the chance to spend our dreams
The way our dreams would seem; to fall
Against ourselves, against us all!

Our dreams were hopes for all the world
When John was murdered, in some dim
November, dim remembered in
The way the world bleeds, at the rim
Of rank misfortune, suffering.

And in the silence of our hearts
There burned a flame that roared and purged
Our fathers of their fathers' sins,
And freed us of our fear, the dirge
Of death was spent in one last surge

Of madness, on some Asian track
Where death and drugs stalked, white and black
And hate were all sequestered there,
The festering sore of all; we were
Determined not to take it back!

Meanwhile the 'yeah yeah' years were just
The outward signs of search among
The minds they drugged from discontent
With all the jingles that they lent, while truth
Was only sung in songs

Of Beatles, and with Beatles came
Fresh hope, long hair, the boy next door
Myth, making it, in making it your
Dreams were dreams for taking, or for
Breaking all that went before!

Sweet songs, beat songs, love songs were all
From you to us, and when you sang
'She Loves You', we believed the score
And married 'til the altars rang .....
Where now the love songs that you sang?

And though we all believed we had
The world wrapped up, the system beat,
The system jived to what we thought was
Our new dream, but all we'd bought were
Variations on some theme!

We fought, by God we fought, I well
Remember, when the flower folk were
Peddling love at hatred's door, in
Hashbury, Haight-Ashbury where
The flowers were crushed and cast ashore.

But times they were a'changing were
Our poet prophets promised us
A share in worlds new-cast in flame.
Our only share was all we spent
In keeping poet profits there.

Still we persevered, we left the
Cities for the virgin soil, our part
Would be the starlit night, our art
Would be the fading light, bleak
Landscapes be our chosen toil.

In final desperation we have
Even resurrected Jesus, time
And time again. But who can pay
The price; six dollars, just for Jesus,
Lights, and all the cast, performed on ice.

If, my children, we have failed, at
Least we failed! The hopes we held
Were never lost, or tossed aside, or sold
To thieves… We failed because the years
Dismayed, and burned the pages of our creed.

6 August 1976

Scrawled Silence

Too often in this gaping land
I've wandered helpless, like some man
Whose art was squandered in the drought,
Bereft within, burnt dry without
Both parched and strangled, word and deed
Cast out from hope, embraced by need
Exiled from all that beauty saw
And lost to all I knew before.

Small wonder, then, that nature's call
Excites me less or not at all,

That harsh intrigues of leaflessness,
And trees grotesque, intrigue me less.
This brown and barren artistry
Calls forth some emptiness in me
To whisper all that sadness seems
And leave scrawled silence, in sad dreams.

7 September 1976

Magic Mushrooms

'The colour has run from your shirt,' I said
'To lie on the churly seat!'
'Too late, too late,' said the surly mate
'To be born of the sworn elite.'
'Your head says – 'cut along dotted line'
And I would, but haven't a pen.'
'The road is right and the day is night...'
You used to be my friend.

'If only you'd taken the turn you did
Before, when it meant so much!'
'Ah, more's the pity and more's the pity
I should have been married Dutch!'
'You should have been shouldn't, and that's a fact,'
I started to disagree,
But caught a glimpse of a glance of mine
Stone dead in my memory.

The face half turned of a friend of mine
And became a wife of his,
But Phil was driving to count the lies
That we'd both tell, after this:

'I've often thought that the time was wrong,
I was born with an evil star...'
But she must have loved you once, I thought,
Then the dash lit up, like a bar!

The bonnet grew and the wheels fell off
And the roar persisted red,
'If all you'd written was all you'd thought,
(Have ever you heard it said),
If half you see is the perfect truth
And half of the truth is lies,
If half of nothing is half as much
Again, and a half surprise...'

'I know... the half of a half-truth is
Only half of the half we see...'
So we both shut up, and we thought of her,
And we looked at the scenery.
'We'll never make it to Hay, you know
At the rate it's moving away...'
As long as she comes away, I thought,
Caught up in some new affray.

'Have ever you really hurt someone
That you loved, as I have done?'
He would have said, but his head fell off
And became a Kitchener bun.
'The trees are back on the march again,
And the moon is wide and free...'
'I seem to have lost my knees,' said Phil.
Her thighs had swallowed me.

'The road is gathering speed,' said Phil,
I thought I could trust you two!
Trust no man in a woman's hand –

I fingered the curlicue.
'We should be there by your birthday, Phil,'
And there was Hay, in the mist,
But I was trying to count the lies
That we'd both tell, after this!

9 September 1976

Horoscope (for Blaise Romany)

These winter days have been long and cold
For the one who waits on the birth in me,
For though she carries the seed I hold
I carry the watchword, 'Destiny'.
The cosmic clock in my loins has set
The future freeze on the planet's race
And what was set by my lovers clasp
Will shine in the new-born spirit's face!

The planets whirl and the planets wheel
To weave their way in the master's web,
I cannot buy, I can only steal
One short life-long at my life-tide's ebb.
The star that falls in the field of wheat,
The lightning flash in the summer storm,
The sigh of shadows, the thunder's beat
Will all be present when you are born!

10 October 1976

Woman In Child

'Oh, woman in child
What dare do you dare;
The wind's in its warren
The rain's in your hair,
The tides of the spirit
Are tides of the moon,
What mysteries ferret
Sweet love in your womb.'

'Womb-woman in child,
What witch do you wear;
Sad King's in his carriage
Wild spell's in the air,
Such wonder has pealed
From you never before,
My child's in your bracken;
My heart's on your shore.'

6 November 1976

1952

The old King lay in the shadow,
The young Queen sat on the throne,
The world half-turned in its sorrow
As I came wandering home!
'Do you mark,' I said, 'the bells,' I said
'There's grief in that mournful ring…'
'They toll for the death of Him,' he said,
'The death of our gracious King.'

My heart lay still in its vestry,
My blood was chilled to the bone,
I carried my books behind me
As I came wandering home!
'We have lost,' he said, 'a man,' he said
'As fine as a man could be!'
'But haven't we lost our King,' I said…
'…and gained a Queen,' said he!

27 November 1976

-1977-

Last Call

I spun the car in a squealing turn
To come to rest by the Olsen gate,
Pumped the pedal and rammed the horn
And yelled: 'You ready? It's getting late!'
The curtain moved in the morning breeze
The door was slammed, and the figure swayed
Across the lawn with a lurch, a wheeze
And down beside in the Chevrolet.

We left the rubber at ditch and bed
A broken rose in the churning air,
'We'd better stick to the coast.'
'You bet!' I didn't want to be seen out there.
A star, set grim in the early sky
To warn of perilous nights ahead:
'By Christ, I've got to get out of here,
I've got to get out before I'm dead!'

'You're out!'
'You bet.' And he heaved a sigh
The sigh you've heard when the world has wept,
The rattling, broken wreck of a lie
That was old when Cain in a paddock crept.
'We'll take the easy Parkinson road,
The road your father, (before he died),
God rest his soul, and the rest beside
The road he took when your mother left.

The startled eyes, at a memory
So old, (when nothing can bring them back)
A flash, a glimpse of a loving face
The date, red-ringed in the almanac.
'It's been so long!' And I knew it had,
We've all discovered the truth before;
'What's lost is lost and it won't be back,
The tide is never the tide you saw.'

I gunned the motor to hear it scream,
The pain of metal is lost on me,
I'd rather the world be drowned in dreams
Than left to mourn in its imagery.
'I've seen your face on a million men
Who fought to conquer the where they were,
You've sought and struggled, and failed again...
'What else could I do - I failed with her!'

The car was drumming a mournful note
On tyres that told of a thousand roads,
The wreck of many a dreaming scheme
Of many a twist and turn, untold.
'You've lost the race, are you glad to go?

There's many a man has lost before,
It's better for those who fall behind
There's only pain at the open door.'

'I've lived with pain!'
'If you stay behind
The pain gets worse as the years are short.'
'And if I go?'
'There's a chance you'll leave
Them all with the thought of what you weren't.'
'There's little choice!'
'But there is a choice,'
I let him think on the things I'd said;
'By Christ – I've got to get out of here,
I've got to get out before I'm dead!'

21 January 1977

Fireflies

(Conceived one night by watching the approaching headlights on a highway in New South Wales).

How sleepless the night!
How your Lords of mischance
Trace their ribbons of light
In some untoward dance.

How cold does he lie,
He, who once, made of man
Traced his final firefly
Through the last of his sand!

What dark rings the eye,
What quivers the hand,
In what cold glows the hearth
By whose word, by whose wand?

How sleepless the night!
When the fireflies leap
In the ribbons of darkness,
By whose light weep?

26 January 1977

Clone

It is not ours to seek to trace
The fall of man, the sharp descent
The sense of some long-lived disgrace
That long-forgotten Man has felt.

Long toppled from some petty star
He called his own, when he began
To call ambition to his aid,
Abandoned God, and worshipped Man.

Brief glimpses only come to mind
Of all we were before the spade
Of Man's misfortune spat the sand
On all achievement's shallow grave.

Before the morning rooster crowed
The end of all the time we had,
The end of chances lost in space
In time, in trust, and lost in sand.

Too late to call forgiveness down
On tortured heads that cry 'repent'
When all the ashes of our kind
Are littered on the sunny strand

Of all that man has built, preserved,
Admired, desired, or bought and sold
Until the stone itself has tired
And crumbled back to dust alone.

'The King is dead – long live the King'
Shall not be heard again from us
Whose litter washes at the breach
Of all we learnt and tried to teach.

The tales were false, the stories told
Were rank injustice, chafing at
The bit of truth we'd lost before
We knew what leash we'd settled for.

But as the shade of death denies
The spark of life its next sunrise,
So knowledge, squandered in the search
For life eternal, in disguise

Destroyed what little life we had…
Poetic justice, if you like,
And all that we, in fact, deserve;
Eternal life is God's preserve!

17 February 1977

Birmingham 1947

My memory's shell-shocked standard flies
Where Birmingham, with red-rimmed eyes
Lay rubbled by my father's house;
The walk-not ways of childhood lay
By walls of shrapnel shattered clay
And rivered screams that coursed to earth
Defied the source of childhood mirth.

The red-brick shelters, haunted by
The smell of fear which, undispersed
By time or fortune, lay within;
The damp, the hollow-echoed cry
Of those whom distant death denied
The justice of the victor's boast:
"We held you at the drowning coast."

The meadow cratered, staggered skies
Cut ragged in the blood sunrise
Await the jagged cross refrain:
"Despair, resign your love of life
Old man, young boy, sad woman, child.
This bloodied reign will pluck such breath
From England's womb to do you death."

Where now the shrapnel of my mind
That caught the first glimpse of my kind
In some bomb-burst, explosive rhyme?
The scars are bulldozed, rubble gone
The seeds of all I issued from,
And fissures only circumscribe
The last of any warrior tribe.

13 March 1977

What Small Dream I?

This dream has ravelled at the edge
Of darkness, since the world turned once,
Before me and behind me
When my spark flared
And dark dared me to ignite!
But the world totters, shattered by
The speed of dreams fulfilled,
And skilled in skills
Not of my delight!

What small dream I, in its
Entirety, could fly in the face
Of fortune, when odds
Greater than eternity
Turn at my cross
And fling life's laurels
At the dreams of other gods?

16 March 1977

The Contract

I see with eyes
Not of my conception.
I steal sighs and weave why's
Wrought from some disaffection with your
Wherefore's and therefore's, and buts
Ifs, ands, hands and thighs.

Am I to lie, dissatisfied
In tides of life's distractions
With your 'what's more's', cricket scores
And less of interaction with your
Lipsticks and silk slips, and knees
Tongue, tights, slights and flaws?

This contract slips
Contrasting inclination
With my part clause, refer yours
Regarding dissipation of my
Needs, pleas, misdeeds, and tears
Ties, lies, sub-para four.

And in the end?
Our last is our disaster
For the dream cries, and love lies
In the bleeding alabaster of our
Silken skins and our lie-ins, where the pain
Pours, the same soars and sighs.

29 March 1977

For Morgan - (my son)

Your way, at last, has gone from me
I see as all the blind can see,
I touch as only beggars touch,
And hear and feel but half as much.

I walk the world in my disguise
To hide the rivers at my eyes
And like a child, in fear I call...
Remember me, or not at all!

For all the planets long conspired
To help me to my funeral pyre,
To tear my children from their mould
And tell them what they'd not be told.

The night that will encompass all
Has rushed to join me in my fall,
To brave the pain that in me cries
This love, that can't be cauterised!

15 April 1977

Vignette

When first cast down, chained to the flesh,
And flushed, unseeing, into this world,
I raged and wept, fought for breath,
Thought revenge on savage nature
Into which my reluctant spirit had been hurled.

My prison, with its carnal needs to slake
Held me close. My mind, weakened by
My earthly frame, whispered: 'forget, forget...'
I have not yet, nor will I
Until my dust relents, and time stores this vignette!

15 April 1977

When the Bomb Goes Off

What y'gonna do
When the bomb goes off
When y'teeth fall out
An' we ain't got Gough?
What y' gonna do
When the bomb goes off,
Will ya tell me will ya
What ya gonna do?

I'll be sittin' pretty
When the bomb goes off
In the old man's cellar
With a glass o' Smirnoff.
Gradually unable
On the old Red Label
To be worried what'll happen
When the bomb goes off.

What y' gonna do
With no Don Dunny
When there ain't no shops
And there ain't no money?
What y' gonna do
When the road's all runny
Will ya tell me will ya
What y' gonna do?

I'm gonna cancel all the
Laws for the livin',
Take the take from the takers

And the give from 'forgiven,
I'm gonna make meself
A brand new flag
An' fly it from a Chevy
Down the ol' main drag.

What y' gonna do
When there ain't no fuzz
An' there ain't no grass
'cos the grass ain't gruz?
What y' gonna do
When ya get no buzz,
Will ya tell me will ya
What y' gonna do?

I'm gonna get meself
A big hangover
Where the high's so high
That y' can't get lower.
Then I'm gonna get meself
A black chequered hat
An' scare all the Cockies
Off the Birdsville Track.

What y' gonna do
If there ain't no chics,
If there ain't no fellas
An' there ain't no kicks?
What y' gonna do
If there ain't no flics,
Will ya tell me will ya
What y' gonna do?

If there ain't no chics
And there ain't no fellas
An' I'm caught dead drunk
In the old man's cellar;
If there ain't no shops
And the grass ain't gruz
And there ain't no money
And there ain't no fuzz.

If there ain't no flics
An' there ain't no Chevy
And there ain't no Cockies
(Now y' really gettin' heavy);
If there ain't no Donny
And there ain't no Gough…
I'll shoot m'bloody self
When the bomb goes off!

13 May 1977

(Note - 'Don Dunny' - Don Dunstan,
Premier of South Australia in the 60's.
'Gough' - Gough Whitlam, Prime Minister
of Australia in the early 70's).

High

I've no use
For your snow or your grass,
Your horse or your hash
Or your stone type trash;
I can get high
On the breeze and the sky,
The storm passing by
And the lightning flash.

I've no time
For your joint or your weed,
Your smack, or the creed
Of the junk you need;
I can get stoned
On a beech or a rowan,
A sail headed home
Or a sunflower seed..

Life's too short
For your H and your coke,
A head full of dope
Or the joints you smoke;
I get my kicks
Where you don't need a fix,
With old-fashioned chicks
And the gentlefolk!

17 May, 1977

The Decision

'You think you can walk away from this,
You think that you're not to blame!
I've a child inside that you've just denied,
But it's your child, all the same.
Yes, it's your young son or your baby girl
That you've just denied - not me!
Or would you prefer to deny us all
Like Peter did - times three?'

'I should have known, you're a lousy lot,
You men - I mean, you boys!
You think that girls are to love and leave
Like the rest of your childhood toys.
Well, I loved you, Tom, yes I really did
And I put my faith in you;
It was faith misplaced, or a lack of taste
To believe in the sketch you drew.'

'I was 'sweet sixteen' and a 'teenage dream'
But I'm nothing else to you,
I'm a 'let's to bed' and a 'silly head',
And yes - I'm stupid too!
How many others believed your lies,
How many others your creed?
How many babies never lived
For the lack of a father's need?'

'You may believe in the 'great reprieve'
If that's what abortion's called,
But your luck ran out when you heard me shout
That you'd just been over-ruled!'

The child is mine, and it will be born,
And it will be loved - by me!
You can go your way 'cos there's nowt to say,
You can go your way - you're free!'

'I'll not be free, I'm in love with you,
There'd be no peaceful night,
But I thought the best for your own sweet rest...
I was wrong - let me say it right!
I want the child and I need your love
But your folks will never see...'
She smiled as she whispered love to him,
'Just leave the folks to me!'

31 May 1977

The Ring-Pull Chain

'It's all I can do to remember
Your face, your look or your smile,
You left one day, but you didn't say
You'd be gone for many a mile;
For many a mile and fortune
That you took in your pocket then,
You left me chained to the window-pane
To welcome you back again.'

'I stared for many a morning,
I cried for many a night,
But kept my pain on a ring-pull chain
I counted by candle-light.
A link for each day you wandered,

A yard for each month you strayed,
Three hundred feet back in Stanley Street
Is waiting to be unmade.'

'You took my love at the parting
But me, you left behind,
My love was never returned, so lost
I followed, travelling blind.
My tears I wove in the ring-pull chain
To save for the day we met,
But steel corrodes, and the old crossroads
Have never been rained on yet!'

'The days of 'sorry' are over,
The long regret's begun,
I came to see if the memory
Would dare to call me 'son'.
If I ever have a child in trust
While life is lost in pain,
I may well go, but my love will show,
And there'll be no ring-pull chain!'

25 June 1977

The Tiger

Do you ever get that feeling that
You're flying, or you're dying, and
You're watching, like it happened once before?
When your mind is rather hazy, or disturbed
And much too lazy to remember where
You saw that scene you saw?

I just get this one returning, like
A ghost that's finished haunting
Other folk, but who has settled now on me.
But I know that I remember that this
Ghost of mid-December was a Terry James
I knew when I was three.

He would start his Triumph Tiger while
Enraptured by the window I
Would watch him in his leathers and his jeans,
Then he'd stroke his tank and wave me, for he
Always called me Davey; 'little Davey'
He would say, for I was three.

And the smell of oily jerkins
Leather jackets, dirty denims would
Pervade him 'til he smelt just like his bike,
Though that throaty Triumph Tiger was much
More than just a bike, it used to roar
When stroked by anyone it liked.

I can see the chrome and trimming, and
The flash of all the women who
Would cling with streaming hair behind my friend,
'Til the day my mother mentioned to my
Father, (who was pensioned), that she
Always knew he'd meet a wicked end.

Then at dusk they brought the Tiger, smashed
And torn, without its rider
To the house that Terry James would see no more,
And the years that followed laid it, let it rust
And quite dismayed it, though I'd jump the fence
To ask it what it saw.

But it answered in its silence that
The end had been so violent in
The sudden shock that tore its metal heart,
That its roar was gone forever, and the
End of a believer made it feel like a
Deceiver from the start.

Now these visions fairly haunt me of
The lad who, not quite twenty, rode
His bike right off his last full-printed page,
For these nineteen years have left me with
His picture, nearing twenty and I
Can't believe he's forty years of age.

When I'm bordering on sixty, then
I know that he'll be with me but
He'll still be dressed in leathers and in jeans;
Then he'll stroke his tank and wave me, and
He'll call me 'Poor old Davey...'
Can't you see - I must know what this vision means!

1 July 1977

Teenage Howl

Do you think that I'm Captain Marvel,
Do you think that I've got the power?
I'm a teenage howl with a hooded cowl
As the whey of the world turns sour.
I'm a puppet, churned in a frenzy
By the battlescars of men,
If I take my place at the end of the race
I'll be left at the start again.'

'Do you think that the great decisions
Are left to the likes of me?
With a zap-pow-zok, the atomic clock
Would banish their pedigree.
But a mere 'Shazam' from a young Batman
Won't challenge the surly throne,
Don't make no wave from your fortress cave
If you want to be left alone.'

'They'll poison your drinking water,
Bombard you with radium 'B',
If you're not insane or in too much pain
They'll hook you on dope or tea,
They'll give you a medical number
And rip off your capital gains,
You'll rust in jail on a bloody nail
And dispose of your own remains.'

'No! I'll be your Captain Midnight
And you can be Joan of Arc,
I've a place in bed for your lovely head
'Til your light ignites the spark;
If you want me out on the streets with you
To carry your placard scowl,
You'd better go bomb the Isotron
And practice your teenage howl.'

26 June 1977

Handsworth Wood

Have ever you seen
On Halloween,
The cloud that covers the trees so green?
The shroud that covers the last of lovers
The shifting mist of the in-between?

I've stood, I've stood,
By Handsworth Wood,
I've stood as long as I thought I could;
All Hallow's Eve is the night I grieve
My Genevieve of the purple hood.

She slipped between
The trees so green,
She slipped from me one Halloween;
The cloud had glimmered, the evening shimmered
But she was never to more be seen.

And since that cloud
Became a shroud,
I've not forgotten the words I vowed;
My patience burns for the cloud's return
To help discern what I might have been.

The day she left
I held my breath,
Her sleight of hand was so very deft;
But Genevieve, I still believe
You'll wander out on some Hallow's Eve.

I wait in vain,
There's only rain,
The rain and part of the cloud remain;
But Genevieve I've not perceived
Since she went tripping in World's End Lane.

World End's Land
In Autumn rain,
There's nothing left of my lost refrain;
For Handsworth Wood is a neighborhood
Where trees are held in a great disdain!

2 July 1977

Father & Son

There is the family photograph
That is your father's face,
There is your father's father
Grey-gathering years apace;
The son, bright-eyed in the morning,
The father, lined and drawn,
The son became the father
On the day that you were born.

We've all set out on the highway
Our fathers wished us well,
The sons became the fathers
In the same distinctive spell;
The road of all beginnings
Is all there is to lend,
But many a twist, and many a turn
Has marred us at the end.

He was my father's father,
I am my father's son,
We've travelled as far, and farther
Than our father's years have run;
The twists and turns of fortune
Mean nothing, lost or won,
But the love of a father's father,
And the love of a father's son.

3 September 1977

Alone

What thought fear burns
Along long lonely, nightlit turns;
With day's light fled
And I, the last long spark
Of reason, crackling on
Through mornings sighed
By mine eye bled.

Alone! The silence stilled
By thought, fought deep to death.
As breath takes pause, considers well
When last may follow next,
Cause master to unmake me
By dawn's drawn bloodless level led.

Rank forms of mornings
Greet cold eyes
Unborn in recognition.
'His eyes are old, gone old, are gold,'

The morning masters said.
Not darkness, but the light I fear;
Her interests swift
Were beached, outreached ...
She left me caught
In death, I said.

12 September 1977

The Minute Measure

The sun dipped into a puddle
The moon burst out of the hill,
His watch had stopped at the junction
And he had sighed at the mill,
The sky was cast in a sullen glow
Like the gleam of steel on the road below
Though neither one did the other know,
Nor ever will!

A mile is a map of fortune,
A yard is a day well spent,
An inch is the minute measure
At the mean of the balance bent.
The silent figure that caught his gleam
Had waited long by the road, unseen
For life is merely a measured dream
Of discontent!

Four thousand beats to the hour
One hundred beats to the mile,
His heart had stopped at the junction
But staggered back at the stile.

The eyes, dim-sighted at life that fled
The mouth agape and the mind that bled,
The sigh that shuddered from one near dead –
Unreconciled!

The car slid over the highway
And slipped away at the verge,
The sun had dipped in a puddle
And slithered away from the world.
The cars rushed by in their surly need
To lose perspective by gaining speed,
Designed to follow, allowed to lead
Some other urge!

Apart is a state of being,
Alone is a man become,
An inch is the minute measure
Of all that a man has done.
He slipped and slid from car to earth-,
(Man has no value, for all he's worth),
And that's the promise we're made at birth
To be undone!

He died on his knees, in wonder
Alone in the traffic's chill,
The road led onto the balance
The moon burst out of the hill,
A mile is a map of fortune
A yard is a day well spent,
An inch is the minute measure
At the mean of the balance bent.

28 September 1977

In The Old Man's House

The mad churl at the headstone,
The vane's point, south,
The bright burn, the sad sin
At the carlin's mouth.
The young field on the old day
By the age-old tarn,
The bloodstone by the highway
Where the wind breasts down;
Athame, set on a black cloth
By the five point star,
The cup brims, the dye sets
By the sharp hoar briar.

The thatch-rot at the damp wall
Of the dark stone hut,
The lampwick at the breastbone
Where the old man sat,
The sharp prick of the hoar briar
The thumb's blood-spray,
The last flickering lamplight
Where the old shades play;
The long slash and the slow hush
At the breath's death joust,
The wind shrieks at red rags
In the old man's house.

20 October 1977

A Waking Dream

Whenever I dreamed, I seemed to set
Some faded poem in motion, yet,
I've only recalled but one vignette,
But one vignette, repeating;

The shadow of one who came to me
On the tide of some deep empathy,
Who beckoned once in her beauty, she
Who came with love, entreating:

'If ever you wake before you sleep
To find the dreams of your future, keep
From looking on, for you may pretend
But never will dreams of the future mend!'

'I am your scheme, your web, the power,
The architect of each sleeping hour,
I fill the pool of your wasted skies
With what will become of your lover's lies.'

'I trip your switch, I flood your mind,
Reveal the future of humankind,
But none of the dreams that come your way
Should ever be seen by the light of day!'

I took her words as another dream
For I couldn't believe the sight I'd seen,
And woke one night before I'd slept
To see where my future dreams were kept.

My nights are bleak, and cold, and chill
For I have stared, and drunk my fill,
And nothing has ever been what it seemed;
I spend my days in a waking dream!

21 October 1977

-1978-

Before a Custody Case

All my futures
Lie heaped upon this hour,
I may not turn at will
For this unfavoured power,
What breath may tip the scales
What long-forgotten word
May turn the certain cause
To my uncertain loss?

My hopes are brittle glass,
My fears are deadly palls
That seek to suffocate
My mind behind their walls.
I may not count the cost
'Til years have past me fled,
Like dreams I left undreamed,
And lives I never led.

16 January 1978

The Kelly Curse

On distant tors, in ancient Keeps,
Where spirits mourn, where magic sleeps,
In meadows wracked by wind and storm
These stones have lain since earth was born.

Long sweeping runes of curse and spell
Forgotten in the earth's slow swell,
Bewitching with some hidden sign
The deeds of sons of ancient line.

Misfortune caught in every step,
Disaster bred with every breath,
From all relief of pain denied
These stones by ancient curses bide.

'Your every son, your every son
Will curse their mothers, every one,
Will curse the day that gave them form,
Will live to see their mothers mourn.'

'And if your line increase in girth
To spread your sons across the earth,
No man may stay, but hunt them down,
Dark death is sweet, the earth is brown.'

'The earth is brown, there's no respite
No cause for them to seek delight,
They'll yield beneath the foreign yoke
Unaided by the gentle folk.'

'In every den, in every nest,
Where sons take sup at mother's breast,
These runes will curse them for their name,
Will call them for some ancient shame.'

On distant tors, in ancient Keeps,
Where spirits mourn, where magic sleeps,
For every son of 'Ceallaigh born,
Old Erin keeps a coffin warm!'

9 February 1978

Mortal Cataracts

What futile webs our journeys weave
When seeking faces, door to door,
Small comfort for some desperate need
To set adrift the sorcerer.
The mirror mocks the memory's eye
The camera captures petty truth
In search of you, the greater lie
Will lie in all I brought you to.

Long waits the man I left behind
Becalmed on some embattled sea,
Since conscience caught his blinkered mind
And left him, contradictory.
I've never lived the play I wrote
Nor caught the curtain in one act,
The blind are blind and so am I
Behind these mortal cataracts!

11 February 1978

One to the Other

There is no fate that
Binds us in our steps,
One to the other,
Caught fast amid the folly
That we spent;
For what, I ask, was folly
In the love for you I lent?

There is no end to
You, or me, for me, or you,
One for the other,
Though years may wheel and turn
To fade at last,
A long light dimly burns;
But flares and flames despairing
At its dying gasp.

No… there is no fate
To bind us in our steps,
One to the other,
No fate or fortune which decrees
This harmony;
Only the wind, playing softly on
The reeds of distant memory.

13 February 1978

Rad Morgan - (folk lyric)

Rad Morgan came riding beside our fair city
All finery, satin and lace,
'Oh where have you come from without your poor Jenny,
And what is that gash on your face?'

'And whose is the horse that you straddle so lightly,
And whose is the bridle you hold,
And whose is the blood on the stirrup, unsightly,
Oh, Morgan, you make mine run cold!'

'Fear not for me, sister, 'twas only a wager,
There's gold in my purse for us all,
But who, I can't tell, he was only some stranger
Who wounded himself in a duel.'

'I'll dress you in only the finest of linen,
In lace, and in silk prettily,
I'll buy you a carriage and line it with deerskin
And you shall go riding with me.'

'Rad Morgan, Rad Morgan, where lies your poor Jenny,
I fear that your maid's come to harm,
New gold for old lies, I would give every penny
If Jenny would only come home!'

'Oh, sister, my Jenny has left to go strolling
Along with the Gypsies of Ross,
To never trust maid with a man who was roaming
I found to my ultimate loss.'

'My brother, my brother, you're pale and you shiver,
What ails, is there aught I can do?
That hound by the meadow is crossing the river
And seems to be looking at you!'

Rad Morgan, he bellowed, and wept in his sorrow,
'That hound and his master, I slew!'
My Jenny was leaving with him on the morrow
And I have slain poor Jenny too!'

Rad Morgan, he rides like the wind in the heather,
His finery's ragged and torn,
And loping some distance behind is the reason
He wishes he'd never been born!'

17 February 1978

Grim Seasons

The sea shore is the gods lap
Where the timeless meet,
The grey ditch by the hedgerow
Is my heart's slow beat,
The dark sky and the crow's cry
And the gulls, slow wheeling,
Are sleep's shroud in a gold cloud
On my eyes, drawn stealing.'

She turned, splintering crystal
In the dawn's brisk chill,
The sharp scatter of silence
By the rook's slow trill;

'I left you for the grey day,
For the cliff's grim seasons,
For the crisp breath, or a life's quest
Of my own small reasons.'

'The long shade of the sundial
For a day's lost thought,
The moon, beamed in a cold room
Where a shadow's caught.
I took flight for the still night
And the earth's slow turning,
For the green hills and the clear rills
And the dream you're torn in.'

21 February 1978

Post Mortem

Some cryptic line has told your time
In words addressed to other friends,
And often pen has poured the wine: Remorse,
To slake the word: Amends;
Your love has won the awful flame
That burns regretful at the breach,
What carping conscience serves as mine
To set your world beyond my reach?

I've told the tale in other plays,
Enacted portions of the dream
But no-one knows completed days that
Seem to seem not what they seem!
You leave some flicker in my brain

That flares impassioned, wantonly,
That dares to whisper, yet again:
'Some part of you is all of me!'

3 March 1978

Wych-Elm

Green is the wych-elm
Torn is the tiding,
Ghosts in the old country
Surely are riding,
Deep lie the shadows
On dull days in waiting,
Trace the old harmonies
Long in creating,
Sharp is the memory,
Dark is the will,
Lost for all seasons
In some rippling rill.

Long did he wander,
He that in I
Took to the meadows,
Gazed at the sky,
Rambled by rivers and
Rolled in the corn,
He that in I was
When we were new-born,
Fled by the wych-elm
Where age and old sin
Awaited his passing
That he would come in.

He that came in as
The I that went by him
Smiled in some greeting
That caught my tongue tying,
Reached for the reins of
His dapple-grey gelding,
Rode through the seasons
That never had ending,
Squandered the meadows
And trampled the corn,
Serving the wych-elm of
Both of us born.

Now I return with
The lines in our faces,
Searching for shadows of
Both of our traces,
Hoping for comfort or
Words of some kindness,
Lost in the echoing
Creed of my blindness,
Shadows of him that I
Tore from within me,
Left by the wych-elm
To steal that he lent me.

Green is the wych-elm
Torn is the tiding,
Ghosts of the old country
Surely are riding,
Out by the meadow
A child that waylays me,

Speaks to me once, and that:
'You have betrayed me!'
Turns at the river to
Gaze at the sky,
Rides away slowly,
He that was I.

Nothing is left for
My bitter eye brightly,
Nothing but shades that
Return to me nightly,
Seasons that flickered, that
Galloped and fled me,
Schemes and ambitions that
Always misled me...
But no-one could ever do
More to dismay me
Than he that was I, saying:
'You have betrayed me!'

5 April 1978

Sir John de Vere

Sir John de Vere has took a quill
And set himself to sit and write
The sweetest love that is of men
To take unto his heart's delight.

And he has took a damsel fair
That flitteth by, beseemingly,
And with a strand of golden hair
Begun to weave her mystery.

The hair it flows from quill to sheet
In whorls and ripples it doth flow,
In twists and bends it eddies forth
To settle on the sheet below.

The hair is sweet in light perfume,
The quill it flows from page to page,
The lady's love has settled there
For all to read and all to know.

The lady's hair has bound her love
With golden tresses to the line,
Her heart is caught, it knows not where,
But may not move, and may not go.

Her skin, that of the lightest hue
Is soft to touch and soft to dare,
Sir John de Vere reveals anew
The secrets of her every where.

The more the pen skims on the page
The tighter are the bonds that bind,
The lady swoons in righteous rage
At whorls and eddies in her mind.

In whorls and eddies it doth flow
The golden hair, a flowing stream,
The cheek is caught and now the thigh,
Imprisoned for the world to know.

'You've made my love a whore', said she
'For all to come and take their sup,
My mind is open, disarrayed,
And so my thighs, my kirtle's up'.

Sir John heard not his lover's plea
But worked from day to night his joy
And took another golden strand
To work his quill another ploy.

And so his muse grew forth apace
His verse became a mighty work
And when his quill had run him dry
He went to seek his lover's face.

He sought and searched him far about
But never no sight of her did see,
Then mused apace before he turned
To seek the pages of his creed.

Among the parchment of his room
He found his love within the scrip',
And all the art and all the grace
He'd taken from his lover's lip.

And all the life and all the joy
Imprisoned on the churley sheet
To leave the shadow of his love
Bereft, and for the world to meet.

Sir John de Vere took on the thread
And pulled it from the final line,
That words that tumbled from his head
Should never not, nor now to bind.

And as the muse its thread was broke
A sigh came from his shadow love,
And colour caught in both the cheeks
And life came back in all the blood.

The arms he loosed then gripped him fast
And lips that whispered him to hear,
He will not write his love at last
Nor never again, will John de Vere.

25 April 1978

Stone Cottages

You built your stone cottages
Without any windows,
No light for your memories
No doors for your soul;
You've long kept your pillages
Deep-dug in foundations
Your meadows and villages
Too far from your home.

The shadows of verities
Loom large on verandahs
To strut at the terraces,
Assault your grim walls;
But all of your sureties
Are locked in your cottages
And all your serenity
In dark, airless halls.

Your lines cross your messages
In treks round old workings,
Your mind lines the precipice
That quickens your pride,
Your darkness is born of

Young dreams and old wreckages,
Short schemes and long yearnings
You've always denied.

23 May 1978

Static

Stark patterns rent by winter storms
Sweep the blood-red sky,
By haunted mills and frozen rills
The static crackles by;
But not a stone stands on a stone
To halt its whispered sigh.

Through twisted steel and molten glass
The signal spends its force
Then mutters on through blackened wheat,
Bent on its wayward course;
But none may hear the crackling tear
That shimmers through the gorse.

Twice round the earth the signal runs
To seek that whip of steel,
The midnight radio of man
Has ceased to hear or feel,
And silence reigns, where once had seen
The skirling of the reel.

In some deep water-filling ditch
Lost in a ravaged land,

The signal finds a radio
Clutched in a dead man's hand;
And crackles static through its leads:
'I have returned, for man!'

9 July 1978

For Erika

It's a weary life, my lady,
And the shadows lengthen so,
We were left in the quiet water
You were caught in the overflow;
Like a raven drawn to the glitter,
Or a moth to the fairy light,
This many a month of winter
Has brought you to mind at night.

Your crystal dreams lie shattered
Your hopes have long been slain,
You're the Queen of your own dominions
In the grounds of your palace – 'Pain';
There's nothing but cold confusion
To take to your bitter bed,
For the words of a distant lover
Lie heavy when love is dead.

But love is a patient healer
And love is our one refrain,
We'll banish your cold confusion,
We'll shatter your palace – 'Pain';
A friend is a hearth companion

That lives in the heart's despite,
Take hold of the love we offer
And live in our hearts tonight.

26 July 1978

Enigma

With what enchanted breath has woman
Whet and whispered man,
To hold him ever-present at her call,
While rolled along the breakers at the
Shoreline of her takers
She has ever kept her shadow to the wall.

For deep in distant caverns with
The comforts of her kind,
The liquid crystal bubbles at the rill,
A word is long defeated, twisted
Shattered and deleted
At some fancy of her puzzle-patterned will.

Long lost in lonely courses where
No ravaged river ran,
I sought to lift the veil of her disguise,
And caught the slow deception of
Her ready recollection
In the substance of the truth behind her lies.

For though her eyes were shutters drawn
Against her inner needs,
I sought the words she never thought to say:

'The icing's bitter-sweet if you
Can only be discreet, but
Never seek to strip my mystery away!'

18 August 1978

Hold As Hold Can

The time shortens
The pace speeds,
Times pile upon times
At the world's needs.

We are the witnesses
At the end spell,
The ranks close rapidly
By the dry well.

You hold the centre,
You guard the flank,
The light but glimmers
Where once we drank.

His deep in hearts
Immune to man,
The last, lost faithful
Hold as hold can.

30 August 1978

Lines on a Mormon Missionary

What sort of wild temptress is this
That tears at the memory's core,
That conjures and courts to dismiss
And knows not what tempting is for?

What softness of speech and of eye
That seduces a man from his lust,
When he knows that he's never to try
But feels that he should, and he must?

And why, in the stillness of night
When the world filters down at the rim,
Does he stare at the long-fading light,
And despair at her image of him?

31 August 1978

Burned Out

The tide has dumped me in some trough
To bleed the longing from my lift
And, like a fool who cries 'Enough!'
I know not where to turn, or shift.
My sails hang limpid in the calm
That burst upon the storm in me
And left me helpless, in alarm,
Burned out, defeated, vanquished me!

21 December 1978

Dyes Cast

Each night
As he drops his head
To the deep dream
Of the dark bed,
A shape beckons him
Wellaway
From the starlight
And the dim day.

A mare
Black as a spade, calls
From the dark hill
As the wind falls,
The reeds mutter
The night is black
As he leaps blind
To the mare's back.

Then like the roar
Of an ill wind
Or a black flame
From the devil's kiln,
The mare speeds
To the night's work
By the old mill
And the dark Kirk.

Shapes flutter
And leap alight
Before they sputter
And, out of sight
Disport and mutter

Of black arts
To see the mare
And the rider pass.

Hour on hour
He clings to scenes
Of dark images,
Wild dreams
And chance friends
From the dead past
In the grim haunts
Of dyes cast.

His face burns
And tears stream
In the long night
Of the dark dream,
He clings grim
To the mare's back
For his soul's sake
And a long lack.

The day brinks
At night's mist;
'There may be nothing
More than this,'
The mare fades
From his wide eyes –
But the thoughts bide,
And the old lies.

'There may be nothing
More than this!'

And his mind seeks
The mare, the mist;
'There may be nought
But the dead past,
And the dark haunts
Of dyes cast.'

27 December 1978

-1979-

Palaces of Glass

'I don't love you anymore!'
Then she turned to face the door,
As the well-spring of emotion burst at last;
For the truth will not be hidden
From the moment that it's bidden
Though it shatters all the palaces of glass!

All the palaces of glass
That we toil to build, alas,
Shatter surely at the first bleak winter's chill;
Along corridors and towers
By the eaves, and in the bowers
Icy winds and bitter mists will take their fill.

'I have loved you now, since when,
And will love, until again
You can find it in your heart to think of me.'
Then I looked, and she was gone
With a winter coming on,
The like of which I thought I'd never see!

Now the night is like a pall
Holding heaven in its thrall,
And the ice has slowed the blood within the vein;
All my palaces are gone
Only memories linger on,
And a love that I could only feel as pain!

24 January, 1979

One Lonely Night

I thought to write of love;
And did, until the critics tracked me down,
To warn me of the blackout in the town ...
No lights above.

No lights above, no voices raised in praise,
No worth in words, no thought for life or love,
But scarecrows that will turn away the birds -
On silent days.

And love then wheeled about,
To threaten of some dull monopoly
To halt my pen and stall my mastery,
And turn me out.

There's little love to write;
Distemper is endemic in the race,
And jaundice is a peril of the eye,
To leave us stare at some receding face ...
One lonely night!

25 January 1979

The Fairy Light

A light appeared on the darkest hill,
The girl fell once, and was left behind,
I caught her arm and we crossed the rill:
'I can't go on - I think I'm blind.'
'We've all been blind to the things that count
But there's the light - if you'll follow me
We may be able to sight the truth,
And catch a glimpse of eternity.'

The light had pranced by the farmer's gate,
Followed the stony lane along,
Leapt a thicket of tangled thorns,
Flashed and fluttered, and bounded on.
'It's only a lonely firefly,
A torch, or maybe a will-o-wisp,'
She clutched her leg and she gave a cry,
I left her there in the morning mist.

'I must go on!' I could hear the words
The wind had snatched at my shallow breath,
'To stay is worse than to venture on,
For standing still is a living death.'
I took the hill like a man possessed
And clawed a way through the cloying weed,
Prayed and whispered and fought for breath
To follow the light of my driving need.

The light had stopped at the stony crest
To turn its wavering glow on me,
I caught it fast in my fevered hand
And felt the light spread instantly.
The hill erupted in seas and stars,

The heavens wheeled and whirled above,
I ceased to be; but whispered 'Why?'
A word, in answer, whispered – 'Love!'

But love like this was not content,
Rather a pit of burning pain,
Only a well of innocence
Could blend unhurt in the light's refrain.
Reflecting the inner glow of love
The great creation wheeled in grace
While I stood dark and shadow-formed,
Apart - as one of the human race!

They found me there at the break of day;
The girl had only a line to tell:
'He must have suffered a stroke', she said,
'His face was pale, and then he fell.'
She didn't mention the fairy light
We'd chased forever across the land;
The girl was lucky - I lost my sight,
And walk the world with a withered hand!

3 February 1979

The Fourth Horseman

I pen this creed for those we leave behind
To scrabble in the ashes and the dust,
And trust my words may touch the shrivelled mind
To find the small compassion we have lost.
No man may cite disclaimers to his fate
When apathy has ruled in dull contempt,
The protests were too slow, and came too late
Were beaten down, were foiled in the attempt.

Each daughter and each son that we have borne
Of perfect line, of perfect form and limb,
Accepted their prerogatives at birth,
The right to life, the right to everything!
The right to bear fine children of their own
To watch them grow, unblemished, in the sun,
But greed has long the seeds of cripples sown,
And monsters have been born to everyone.

Since ever peasants tired of bitter bread
And stormed the battered fortress of dissent,
The avarice of man has set the tone
Of everything the newfound masters lent;
And we must share our burden of the guilt
And count it to our cost, the grim mistake,
That peasant minds, indebted to the hilt
Were offered bread, but turned to yellowcake.

A people with no moral sense must fall
Who can't control the rage of deadly toys,
And forfeit, for the overpowering pall
Respect and life, and see them both destroyed.
We said - 'It: doesn't matter, give us work,
The world will leave us steadily behind...'
If only all the world had gone ahead,
But finally, the blind advised the blind!

6 March 1979

After the Bomb...

'Goal!' he yelled, and laughed up at the sun,
And gambolled on the lawn in his delight:
'United leads by seventeen to one - '
His father smiled, but marked the fading light.
The boy went tiger-hunting in the grass,
And called for Gyp, who lay awhile and slept,
'You lazy dog – come out and join the fun!'
But Gyp, a long slow silent passage kept.

Another volley passed between the two
Who laughed, as if the world had time to run,
A hollow ball, filled tight with empty air
That soared and shone, to imitate the sun.
'If centre-forwards came from outer space
And kicked the Earth – a penalty – to Mars...'
His father sighed, and turned away his face:
'What man can hope to understand the stars?'

Then silent, in the middle of his stride
The man half-turned, and fell, and hit the earth;
Rolled over on his face, and then he cried...
But soundlessly, beside the youngster's mirth.
'So now you've seen me fall,' his father said,
'I'm fallible, like any other man...
All men can make mistakes,' he bent his head
And gazed in silent wonder at the land.

'I've only ever acted out of love!
You must believe...' he faltered, and was still,
The lad reached out and touched his father's hand
As silence settled on them, like a chill!

The boy walked on ahead a little way,
To spare the hand that trembled on the gun...
And thunder! And a peaceful summer's day,
And anguish, and an end to everyone.

15 April, 1979

Yellowcake

I've seen it in the mirrors that
The fleeting death-wish speeds
From ugly strangers tugging at the lie,
If they're to be dismembered
From the vision, since remembered
Then that vision, surely, touches you and I?

The corridors are endless in
The palaces of power,
And islands are forbidden by the law,
But life shall be extended
At the instant it's defended
Though the traitors pack their dollars at the door.

The mighty mausoleums
In the images of man
Have wracked this sorry planet to the core,
And background radiation
Is the heart's-blood of the nation...
Though the heart just isn't beating anymore!

24 April 1979

At Eaglehawk Neck

She moves within
The rapid dream
That seeks to spill
Her tangled skein,
And touches others
Barely seen
Who shadow-pass
Another's pain.

The waters lap
Her anchored feet,
The forests turn her
To the shore,
The whirling tide's
A skirling scream
That spins her helpless
To the floor.

By some embittered
Candlelight
Her pen describes
The blackest line,
To tear the slender
Thread of night
In some despite
Of Valentine!

24 May 1979

Sea and Shore

Why do you tear at
My towers and my turrets,
My walls and my pillars
My barrs and my beach;
And mutter like musings
Of untoward poets,
And scatter your silences
Out of my reach?'

'Why do you surge and
Assault in your anger
The fortress I built for
My lady asleep,
And slowly dismiss each
Dispute you remember
By wearing each stone
From the base of the Keep?'

'What is the torment that
Claws at the crofters,
The meadows, the rookeries
Close to your door,
And where is the mistress
As sweet and as soft as
The ripples you listlessly
Waste by the shore?'

'I'll balk and I'll beat
At your very foundations,
I'll tear down your turrets
And pillars of stone,

The lady that sleeps at
The edge of my oceans
Was mine when your acres
Were torn from my throne.'

'But time has not told
All the tales of my fathoms
And constant I am
To the love that I keep,
Each year I assault and
Encroach your dominions,
Your towers and your turrets,
Your castle and keep.'

'Long may you surge and
Assault my defences,
Beat in your anger
At granite and slate,
The lady that sleeps has
No further pretences,
Your labour of love
A millennium late.'

'Now shall I fume at
My lady's defection and
All her deceptions
From headland and Tor,
Love is as false as
Your petty foundations
When love may be left
Beating up on the shore.'

28 June 1979

In Retrospect

When all the threads are broken,
When all the vows are spent,
When every word that I've said or heard
Means only ... I repent!
When all the ships of fortune
Have sailed to a foreign strand,
I'll give my memories, every one
To hold you by the hand.

When yesterdays tomorrows
Hold nothing more for me,
And all my fate and fortune
Is lost in my imagery,
When every friend and favour
Has turned to walk away,
I'll watch you from my window
Act out the ragged play.

When all the futile speeches
We've made to each and all
In search of some dim purpose
To save us from the fall;
When all the futile speeches
Hang dust in the empty air,
I'll need you more than ever
To tend my dark despair!

June 1979

Words

If all my words
Were scattered on the sand,
To mingle with
The acres of the sea,
Just four I'd keep
To hold you at the hand...

My woman now:
'Grow old with me!'

1979

Stars

Soft-scattered at
The dark side of the earth,
Before the dawn -
Horizoned at the beam
  of feathered sunlight -
Pricked me at the touch;
The stars fell.

And every star
In falling at my hearth
As day awoke,
(Its slow advancing seam),
   The precious, flickered phantoms
   Turned to dust,
   While snow fell.

The children cried,
Delighted at my dearth,
As morning caught
The star in every dream,
And melted every snowdrop
Into rust,
At eve's knell.

And once the petty
Glow that we disperse
Has flickered at
The act we can't redeem,
May sudden sunlight
Sanctify our trust,
In Noel!

2 August 1979

Home-acre

Is this your home-acre
Dark beauty of mine,
Cold winds and rash words
And long hurts and harsh wine,
Caught fast in disasters
That seldom relent,
Am I your un-maker
My sweet discontent?

Is this your home-acre
This bleak, loveless tor,
Where promises are lost in
The dreams on your shore,

Where all that you hoped for
And wished for your own
Was left in harsh soil with
The seeds that I'd sown?

6 September 1979

Tack & Edge

I stand marooned at life's most distant shore
With all the old eternities behind,
And face the frigid future's cold attack
With all the faded blessings of the blind.
What frown has laced my narrow path across
What distance set apart the me from mine,
What rank disaster stands between
The water and the wine,
Or falls between the dreamer and the dross?

A step may drive me onward to the void,
Or poise me at the brink of certainty,
Where oceans tack and edge this ragged world
To draw me in to some deep verity.
A storm may cast my life and love adrift
To leave this weary sentinel alone,
What acres lie between me and
The rolling of the stone,
Or sound the shallow waters of your shift?

9 September 1979

Late of Days

What have you left me,
Late of Days?
There's never a smile
For my words of praise,
And not a look
Or a sigh is spent
To point the way
That the wonder went;
Where is the way
Of the ancient ways –
What have you left me
Late of Days?

What have you left me;
Tardy nights
And grim repairs
To the look-alikes,
A heart that's troubled
And torn, and spent –
Which was the way
Your wishing went?
Why these thoughts
Of your witching ways –
What have you left me
Late of Days?

25 October 1979

-1980-

Poverty Grass

Wild horses we
Pricked at the wind,
Never to know - alas;
That all the lord of our fortunes bought
For us
Was poverty grass.

Poverty grass
The paupered seed
So sickly poor - alas;
The souls of the great untamed grow weak
Despair
On poverty grass.

And you, my friend,
Grew sick awhile,
And cried and cried - alas;
While I grew fat on a flowering weed
Called pride
And poverty grass.

And when you left
The field to me
I almost died - alas;
For I was left in a fallow field
Piled high
In poverty grass.

Wild horses we
Pricked at the wind,
Never to know - alas;
That all the lord of our fortunes bought
For us
Was poverty grass!

24 January 1980

For Leslie… (A 21 Year Old Divorcee)

The past is neatly shed!
The long mistakes and distant heartaches
Trail no longer to your bed.
Fortune waits with bated breath
To promise you such better things,
Chrysalids yield butterflies,
And butterflies reveal –
        Bright Wings!

2 February 1980

Milady Gay

Milady Gay, whose
Breath is like a sin,
A sin, to sit upon
The light within,
Within;

The light that fractures
Forces, forswears
The race we run –
While wracked, backed and put upon
We face the face we
Trace our stencils in;
And vent our sated discontent
By pencilling our demons in.

Milady Gay, see
Not the sin in sin!
For love, lust, life, sight
Shine brightly in
The times we briefly spin;
While touch, taste, pace
Haste and promise deal
With chastity at last,
And love's hood delights all
In tight cauls at life's kiln.

9 February 1980

Port Hughes Revisited

The sand remains, but naught, my love, of you;
Our dancing shadows tilted at despair,
For everything my love required of you
Convinced me that I'd caught and kept you there.
But emptiness in me is like the weed
That devastates the long and lonely beach,
While shadows of your sadness and your need
Continue dancing onward, to the breach.

1 May 1980

For a Dreamer

If all I gave
Was dust for dreams
To leave tall shadows
In short schemes,
If all I left
Was brief regret,
Then may your dreams
Be dreaming yet.

But if I lit
Some star in you
To light those eyes
That sought me, too,
Then surely all
Was not forlorn...
Such dreams are but
Of dreamers born!

7 May 1980

Before The Storm

If only I
Had caught the hand
That tore the shroud
And split the wand
To scatter pain
Across the land...

If only You
Had pulled the thorn
Of all my dearth
From in me born,
Or stripped your pride
Before the storm...

If only we
If only we
Had loved enough
To halt and see;
If only we...

20-21 May 1980

Brick by Brick

In every word, in every smile
We distance drift a further mile,
By every whispered fare-you-well
You brick by brick our wishing well.

In every loving touch, or kiss
The seed will start my heart to miss,
And every time you touch his hand
My blood lies weeping on the land.

In every soft and sweet caress
Despair will feed my wilderness!

2 June 1980

Threads

With all the art of patient mending
First this thread, and then that binding,
Now this stitch that, so demanding,
Spilt the verse I caught your mind in;
On to scattered words of wanting
Gleaned from needs and shadows, haunting;
All is lost that you believed in –
Leaving love for me to grieve in.

Now I sit and want and weave in
All the dross of bitter lendings,
New beginnings from old endings!

11 June 1980

Grasmere

(From Dorothy Wordsworth's Grasmere Journal – October 6th 1800.
'Monday. A rainy day. Coleridge intending to go, but did not get off.
We walked after dinner to Rydale. Determined not to print Christabel
with L(yrical) B(allads).'

I

Of all the lines
You wrote in haste
Before the dream
Was laid to waste;
With all the trappings of your spell
You wove the lay of Christabel.

Sweet Christabel, and Leoline
Whose stern and unforgiving mind
Had forged the feud with Tryermaine;
How Geraldine, the fulsome wench
Would brave the toothless mastiff bitch
To cast some all-enchanting spell –
(Jesu, Maria, shield her well),
Upon the breast of Christabel.

And now she fixes with her eye
And now she stands and stares aloft,
And though the dead all sleeping lie
Still Geraldine will whisper, soft
At some unseen but seeming host
That at her birth, our lady lost.

And now, entreating: 'lie abed
While I seek footsteps in my head,
And pray for your Sir Leoline…'
Thus spake the wiley Geraldine
Who, letting fall her silken dress
She turned to Christabel her breast,
Bewitching with half-naked side
The maiden who abed had lied
To watch this sight, so long denied.

II

At what point in their dull applause
Became the thought a certainty
That this in print must never be?
Were there lines that took the breath
From this austere togetherness –
As: 'Christabel then gave her breast
To some long-lingered, sweet caress?'

Then as the wanton, Geraldine,
The daughter of Sir Leoline oppress'd,
She ran her fingertips
Across the moist and maiden lips
Of Christabel, exquisite pain -
We walked to Rydale, in the rain.

And when her maiden thighs were spent
With all that Geraldine had lent
The lady Christabel lay still,
Deep murmured in some hidden rill,
That stole across her countenance
And took the place of innocence.

III

And in the morning, drizzle rain
That beat upon some window pane
Saw Coleridge in Grasmere pent;
While Christabel lay late abed
To footsteps, sounding in her head –
Then took to paper, pen and ink
And wrote – 'Determined not to print.'

14 June 1980

My Daughters Dear

The worlds I sought and thought to win
Have slipped so far, my daughters dear;
I loved and lost them, every one,
They turned away and left me here.

The mere of memory runs deep,
And dark the depths, and chill the shore,
While those we love are often left
To perish at the warm heart's core.

For every step aside we stray,
For every hurt, and every gall,
We lose the thread that marks the path
Between each other, and the fall.

And those we love will often turn
To tear at us in bleak revenge,
For some omission, dim perceived
That pencils 'finis' at the end.

So if I miss your growing years
And all the sound of laughter near –
Tear not the web I wove you through,
I love you still… my daughters dear!

22 July 1980

Bad Blood

Stars clash, and pale moons
Gloat over you, my pretty witch
While brooding shadows of the loom
Reflect you in some shining dish;
What vivid patterns of despair
Have you designed to harness me
Within the ever-changing snare
Of your disingenuity?

Your rage has torn the tattered storm,
The sheeted sky I crawled beneath,
While slatterns, with some jealous dye
Have stained us, injudiciously;
Of all I left behind in you
Some slim deceit has marked your moan
To wean you from disloyal truth
And cast you from your tragic throne.

Embattled clouds stretch you ahead,
Gales whip you onward, as before
The tides conspire with your desire
To drive against a dismal shore;
You sit astride the wreck of dreams
Like some grim ruin, at the flood

To loose the rusted anchor seams
And leave sad tidings, in bad blood.

29 July 1980

Against The Rain

My lady, you once sought my drift
When all the world was scatter-pain,
And in the shallows of my shift
You turned my face against the rain;
(You caught my trace in your refrain).

Word-weary in remembrance,
Embittered by a long distrust
I thought that love was some mischance
That tears and time would turn to rust;
(To leave us bleeding, as it must).

But you long drained the bitter cup
That saw me tortured at the lip,
While I divined at thigh and sup
The virgin grace that gave me sip;
(You loved me at the lowering lip).

If only care is all we find
While forging links to make the mend,
The long disasters bought in kind
May not affect the way we spend;
(And love may win us, in the end).

23 August 1980

Surge

At Granite Island's seaward side
We sat, and watched the surging tide,
The rapid rip, the capping crest,
The stinging spray, the ragged nest;
The long slow wheel of the sea bird, moaning,
The deep-felt urge of the white sea, foaming.

You laid your head on me, and cried:
"How long, how long?" And I replied:
"This day is ours, and for the rest….
Ah well," I sighed, and sought your breast;
You turned, long-lost at the deep shades forming
While I caught tears at the tip of day, dawning.

12 October 1980

On the Passing of My 36th Year

What
Brings this or that to here,
To loss, or spare
At these, my racked foundations?

Each tumbled brick, spilt
From toppled spires,
Where tired lies tell all guilt
Despairs
At the kindle lent
By night fires.

What pennants flung
From yard and mast in youth,
When grapeshot, ball, chain and truth
Spat,
Heeding not, my dear...
That frail craft
Time;
My privateer.

Years along, grey, drab and grim lipp'd
Salt taste and beard,
I would I'd waited there...
My Guinevere!

24 November 1980

On the Death of John Lennon

This world unravels, bit by bit
Each thread that binds
Is torn in rage,
And desolation stalks where wit
And beauty walked
On some lost page.

From light to darkness; life and art
And talent bleeds
At every loss,
Each shallow murder strikes the heart,
The root, the branch,
The Saviour's Cross.

Now at the height, some furtive thief
Has stolen yet
Another strand,
And left in thrall unyielding grief
To wonder at
This bloodied hand.

10 December 1980

Contage – (a conversational montage)

We stared the night at stars, as in a dream
That one might fall, to prove that we were real,
And show the world the order of some scheme
That we had launched, to tip the earth aside,
Beam-ended, tripped and floated cobweb wide
Where none before had thought to see or feel.

Then as we stood, they beckoned us to them,
They beamed the waste that tricked us into flight
While conjured with the bitterness of men
We sensed what none of us could ever see
As long as Mars, unconquered in your tree,
Remained to set afire the pitch of night.

'But surely, you have caught some puny stars
On canvas, where you trapped them with your brush,
As I have scrawled and inked the train of Mars
In manuscripts, on envelopes and leaves
Enough to stay the mind of man that grieves
His violence, once the world has turned to rust?'

'Too late,' you said, 'for time is running out,
And we, two puny souls, are not enough;

The world will rush, like lemmings, to decease,
Before the robber barons slake their lust!
For gilt and gold and oil sate their creed,
While art and grace and culture turn to dust!'

31 December 1980

-1981-

A Welsh Hymn

Bron Dilys Teashop
Of Threadneedle Alleyway,
Swaddled in a pinafore
And cosseted in lace,
Soon charmed the borough boys
When she sang long for the scallywags
Or served up sweet tyshan lap
With her famous welsh cakes.

Her soft-breasted menu
Of cariad and comfort,
Her short tacky temper
Emblazed her blue eyes,
Dai Jones ate those long legs
Alive in the bara brith
And deep-delved her laverbread
With his brandysnap lies.

Then was Tilly Tongue-fit
Sweet cuddled in the marigold
With muddling Tom Tiddle-O

And his calico cat,
Dan Rees called for 'cave-o'
As Tom stoked the middle-up
To watch for the Billy Boyo
And Moll Thunderclap.

Long years now I've wondered
At the conjure of your alleyway;
Does Bron Dilys Jiggle-O
Still sup bara caws,
Does Willy the Wag now
Still wriggle in the coal-hole
With a mouth full of marigolds
And a handful of yours?

I spend my mind dreaming
Of cariad and comfort,
Of tight fitting pinafores
In parlour and bower,
Her bonnet up-ended
In the spell of welsh rare-bits
Sweet tasted, willy nilly-o
Back when, in Bryn Mawr.

19 February 1981

Vain Imaginings

We have grown old
Time will not wait
For us, who caught
Its drift too late,
Who spent like fools
And lent like Kings
Purblind with vain imaginings.

For though each cup
Would spill the brim
At every sup
Of every whim,
What fool could see
His own intent –
Each shallow draft the level spent.

And now, like beggars
Caught in need,
We hoard the dregs
Of every creed
And only taste
The waste of Kings
Purblind with vain imaginings.

1 April 1981

Party Trick

What long dread phantom
Of lost ways
Could trip your cause
To weep your want
When I have sought
Un-numbered days
For all that you
In conscience lent.

No slight despair
Could wake your need
Before I tressed
Your loss in dream,
And no cold comfort
Bought your creed,
And no pretence
Your essence gleaned.

For you lent ravage
To your grace
By cutting men
With every quick,
You veiled each aspect
To my trace,
And laid in waste
My party trick.

15 April 1981

Pas De Deux

Who can say when all this was begun,
The leaping shadows, darting at the dawn,
The silent moods, dispersing, one by one
And metal figures, straining at the sun.

Which birth was which, and who and how, you said,
And why and when; you name each nameless grief,
But will she dance the woodland once again
To pas de deux with every falling leaf?

For she, who bore you in some hidden mould
And beat her anvil silently within,
Who, restless, turned you out to meet the cold
And sought her own vast silences again…

This one has caught you tugging at the heart
And fled within to hide her disarray,
She spoke the psychic tongue of one apart
To set you questing, restless at the clay.

For you have forged and wedded at the flame
How many wings to help man into flight?
Each twisted, turned and engineered in pain
In some attempt to set his mind alight.

Your women, neatly halved between the thighs
Expose the rhyme that you could never win,
And bare the pristine agony of lies
You wrote, before you gave away the pen.

And thus the one that tears the living light,
That bares each sinew, clawing at the scream,
What distant horror fled you by the night
To lend your hand to some one other's dream?

What lifelong silence taught the child by rote
That all of life was bound in petty rape;
If harsh despair could catch us by the throat
In what would lie the seeds of our escape?

Escape from what – from time that lines each face
And limits every man upon his quest,
To cage the soul within each planet's trace
While she performs some careless Arabesque;

While she disturbs each beaten man of steel
Who burns to raise his wings against the spell,
For she has wrought the silence that you feel
And none may gauge the fathoms at her well.

23 April 1981

A Canticle for Wakeman

A few short lines informed us you were dead,
That at the last you'd spent your destiny
The battle, so one-sided at your bed
With no relief for faded dignity.

But no false platitudes to bear, thank God,
No long recriminations for past deeds,

Not one to care, not one familiar head
To ease the passing spirit of its needs.

For some is death the only guarantee
That hell's short tenure may be set aside,
That misery, and want and charity
May be consigned to someone else's pride.

When, long rejected by the ones we love
We face our insecurities alone,
What moral should we draw upon for those
Who, faultless, judge for what we should atone?

I feel at one with you, for in the deed
I too have failed too often for success,
The same bleak planet I have known and grieved
Took you along a lifetime of distress;

And found you grim, unwilling to accept
That laurels should pay some one other's fee,
When you had bled your way from debt to debt
And paid full price for wounds they wouldn't see.

So rest your head, I should have said it yet,
That someone cared, and why, and so much more,
When you had need, and I had no regret…
But then, I should have said it all before.

1 June 1981

The Sentinel

(Imagine a four sided figure which is spinning slowly clockwise - Each panel may be read down,
or entire piece may be read across)

I STAND	ALONE	THAT	YOU ARE NOT
ALONE	IN THIS	MY FRIEND,	THE ONLY
ENDURING	BLINDNESS,	IS A BLEAK	WEATHERED
THOUGH	EVER VIGILANT	AND CALLOUS	SENTINEL
UNWILLINGLY	I OBSERVE	APATHY	THAT WILL
ADMIT	NO GUILT	WITHOUT	DESPAIR
THAT ALL IS LOST	OF MAN'S	ACHIEVEMENT	AND HOPE
-	-	-	FOREVER

6 June 1981

To an Artist

When I first saw your lady kneel
In self-content, before the glass
Some chord of long delight decreed
That I must see her maker's face.

And so we met, my friend, and then
Some alchemy was born in need;
Your art adds magic to my spell,
My words give meaning to your creed.

Now for each hour you spend alone
With painful themes that I have wrought,
Your art disturbs my very dreams,
Your figures rule each line I wrote.

In some unseen far future, they
May say we once brought long delight,
That we burned candles through dim hours
At either end of our midnight.

25 June 1981

Time Knows No Passages

Nights in white cottages
By the last of the flickered firelight,
Supping sweet pottages
To the wind-wail without,
With the water on the wet wall
And your shadow on the lattices
As you cold-come to comfort
In the red candlelight.

At the grey day's frail dawning
We walk the storm ravages,
We talk at the tattered sea shore
Where the tide night-high rips,
I kissed you on a grey sky
Where the shells turn to sea-sand,
For time knows no passages
At a warm woman's lips.

5 July 1981

Careless Lines

Must I forever take the past
And cut it from my heart,
Appease the green-eyed goddess of your whim,
And make believe that nothing
Ever touched the finer part
Of that man who cast such careless lines from him?

Must I be always sorry
For the things I said and did,
Apologize for all you never knew,
And live for every moment
That your pride would have me bid,
To leave nothing in the past for me or you?

I think it would be better
If we cherished all we'd had,
Not caring if despair once closed the door,
For life casts shadow patterns
That may turn from good to bad
At the instant that we think we've won the war.

So if the pattern darkens
Or the sun begins to set,
And the future's lost to all that we have felt,
You may think back on me kindly
And deliver some vignette,
That might the hardest heart begin to melt.

5 September 1981

Five Children I

Five Children I
Once helped conceive,
I watched them grow
I watched them leave,
And each one left
A wound in me,
And some left two
And some left three.

And now when I
Cry out in pain
There's not one left
To call my name,
There's not one left
To grieve for me
Though I wept through
Each history.

But when they grow
They may conceive,
May learn to know
What wounds we leave,
And think back on
Some long despite
When I lay staring
Late at night.

2 October 1981

Sonnet - on My 37th Year

This thirty-seventh year is made complete
Of endless days, and longer nights misspent,
For every year not stormed and racked by argument
Leads on toward some long-drawn, dull defeat.
And so we word and weed away the days
Each hour remorseless in its will to waste,
The only judgement travels with due speed
To leave us death, and careless government.
So while each word is breath, I'll be content

With such a year as this has been again,
Each due was paid, and somewhere in between
The time was put to better use, and spent;
For what I hoped was done, and well done all the same,
To win the love of one well worth the name!

22 November 1981

1981

This broken year
Waits tinseled, brinked
At held breath
In hard times,
To drain some favoured
Harlot's drink
And stay death
With coarse rhymes.

What principle
This wanton cost
Or short sold
For long Lust,
And what price
Your cheap gilt,
And where Lost
Lies all trust?

Each winking tree
Blinks blind, alone
Across and back
Each barren verse,

Where chrome wheels
Seek warm hearths
As Christ drives
His cold hearse.

8 December 1981

-1982-

Where Cobwebs Line

No longer young, I trace my spin
From youth towards this mirror's edge,
Where dour despair is caught within
Or poised, at some forbidding ledge.

For what was lost is not perceived
Beyond each tarn that checks the stream,
We flow from grace to age, deceived
By echoes, in some anxious dream.

And justice, truth and light has been
Forgotten in the twisting skein,
Where cobwebs line the mirror's sheen
To trace faint patterns at my name!

26 January 1982

Danse de la Mort

(This addresses a woman who escaped from an Institution during a snowstorm, and was found the following day buried in snow).

When you were first deceived beyond your trust,
Was death, to you, some god-forsaken tryst?
The blood your mother coughed, a brief disgust,
As she caught life's rank poison at the breast?

Did every spot that stained a dress of white
Give white some deathly horror of its own,
And when you heard the cough catch every night
Did you see death at tryst between each moan?

The final shroud, when she no longer bled,
When she no longer breathed, was deathly white,
Unspotted by the imagery she fled,
In peace, she entered some eternal night.

To leave you caught in torment at the pain
Before your father turned, to walk away,
Some long desertion caught you at the brain -
But whose the guilt, and who would have to pay?

For some is life a short and turbid dream
Who have no will to read beyond the rote,
Each instinct seems sufficient in the stream
That renders every spirit destitute.

And every depth and deep is chained within
To gain control of depths beyond despair,
Though some have nothing worth their while to spin
Once every love has taken of its share.

But what desertion triggered your retreat
To send you spinning, backward through the years,
Did love withdraw, and leave you incomplete,
Or did he fade, and turn his face to hers?

And as each image tilted at your tithe
Did you retreat forever, running blind,
To spare the thought of what you were alive,
With death ahead, and death long left behind?

Until, with reason flown and fluttered wide
You tripped a gentle pas de deux with death,
And as the snow submerged the countryside
What imagery ran trysting at your breath.

What beauty ranged beyond your fading eye
As snowflakes fluttered, whirling at your grace,
To cover some last falter at the sigh,
As peace stole long and lonely, at your face.

7 February 1982

The Pen

'All curses on this pen,'
I see you think,
This dark intruder that demands
Its pint of ink;
It leaves harsh trails and seeks to
Imitate the past,
Though never moves,
But leads the eye toward the glass!

For as the trail goes out
From birth to death,
A black unbroken scrawl
To steal the breath,
It steals the art
Of conversation's better side,
While you look on
Like some poor, jilted bride,
Who has the well,
(If I but had the ink),
And dips me well
When I do cease to think!

22 March 1982

You and I

If life was only
Held at hand
To seize, let fall
Or pass us by,
With every day
Beyond recall,
We'd still remember,
You and I;

We'd still remember
Days of Grace
That gave us peace
Beyond the lie,
We'd still recall
The calm sea,
The boat, the bay
And you and I.

9 April 1982

Before the British Fleet...

Before the British Fleet sailed out
At this despite
Like one last lonely, errant knight
For chivalry,
Three hundred years set all
This rabid world alight,
Then slowly faded,
Like some tainted tapestry.

Three hundred years hang all
Upon this lonely hour,
Each generation tugs its children
At the blood,
To whisper 'pride' at each and every
Listening ear,
That every tide and time be caught
Before the flood.

But as the cynic world
Now stands aside
To see this final far-flung tilt
At mastery,
Who waits as breathless as
The autumn bride,
While time sits trembling, at the edge
Of history?

9 April 1982

The Basic Tenets

The basic tenets of my faith
Remain, though time has blunted all
The finer points I once embraced
By casting doubts beyond my trawl.

For now a sober Saturn sets
Its nets at my small sanity,
While I remain obsessed with things
That ravage this mortality.

Time teases man a little way
Then casts him out, adrift in space
As if his grace were nothing blessed
And all his dignity but waste.

And it is this that most appals
The cultured mind, the man within
Who weaves long patterns through short dreams
That he conceives, but may not spin.

That he conceives, and yet must leave
In ruin at his final breath
While others pick his patterns clean
And tread, like him, his dreams to death.

13 April 1982

2May82 - The Falklands

We, who may but sit and fret
In impotence, while you would dare
Would brave the battle with you yet
If chance had only set us there.

We each have Vulcans of the mind
To harbour some dark manhood in,
But like the bat that flutters blind
We trust in dreams we cannot win.

And when each day's short course has run
And dreams lie scattered at our feet,
We think of all we might have done
And join, at heart, your battlefleet!

2 May 1982

All Things Burn Slowly

All things burn slowly
Dim
And I
Like one whose sight
Is failing him,
Turn inward at the widening gyre
To moth-drawn brightness, and desire!

Each ragged impulse
Spurs
While we,
Caught up in life's
Enchanted verse
Score some soft lonely, passing beat
While dactyls trip each slim deceit.

'Til life has fled us
Long,
They may,
Who did but know
When right was wrong,
Find all is echoes and refrain
Where gods once tapped each window pane!

10 August 1982

Tennos pour Lorac

I find it strange that one as versed as you
In discontent, and having such small time
For poets, or the matter of their muse,
Would make it such an issue of the mind
To lose a book, no matter how it went;
Misplaced, or left behind, or even tossed
On this, the rubbish-heap of dreams long spent,
Before the love that brought the book was lost.
For sonnets, after all, speak love to those
Who still may love, so what would you with these?
- Torment each page that it might ever close
On something you so carelessly dismiss?

I bid you, let this persecution cease...
I do not have your 'Sonnets from the Portuguese!'

16 August 1982

On the Execution of a Mural
by Allan Todd, concerning the Battle of Maldon.

Dim figures from the mists walk at my wall,
Emerge and turn and point and tear them free,
From some white back-washed landscape overall,
That you have etched beyond, so patiently.

For every stroke discovers some old ground
That Saxon rode, or Viking trod before,
And from my well of words your brush has found
The distant vista of some wilful war.

The war we're waging still, the spirit seems
To chafe at limitations in the plan,
Each striving after what we know of dreams,
Is overcome by flaws in every man.

For as you peel each layer from the wall
Disturbing truth as it may lie beneath,
Your brush reveals each want these figures trawl,
Relives the last that loss would see them breathe.

Each stroke I see as tearing at their shroud
While they emerge, so wilful in the mind,
I almost hear the clash of armour, loud
Though every staring eye is dead, or blind.

As blind as we who, trapped within our time
May not remove ourselves beyond the page
That we forlornly pattern with our kind,
To pen each failing foray of our age.

For as each man will struggle to emerge
From white, to take his shape from his surround,
And hope to be embodied at the dirge
His death, a thousand years, will run aground;

Then so may we, who taunt the living clay
And heedless of the time we hold in trust,
So struggle from the bonds of our dismay,
Before the mural moulders at our dust.

But though we may, dim figures from the mists,
Emerge and turn and point and tear us free,
Once history has sealed us at its lips,
Some brush might etch our canvas differently.

29 August 1982

On the Raising of the Mary Rose
From the waters of the Solent - 11 October, 1982.

Long since I sailed me
I and 'Great Harry'
Pride of the ragged fleet
When we were merrie,
Heel at the wind, my tars,
Gunports at ready.

There sat the Frenchman
Here, our great ships,
Hard on the helm we are
As the port dips,
Long cries of 'Mary Rose'
Die on their lips.

Deep-dredged these centuries
Now wedged on high
Stark, as my timbers
Wide-arc the sky;
Where now 'Great Harry',
Where does he lie?

Torn from my bitter-rest
Borne to your day,
Wide-eyed and wild is my
Sad disarray;
Tell my 'Great Harry' now –
Your world is grey!

14 October 1982

Beyond the Breach

If he once knew the light, it has not been
Self-evident, since he first turned and ran
Headlong for some despite he caught alone
Against the loveless brick of Birmingham.

For somewhere in the swell and moan he heard,
Before the velvet sac was ever breached,
Some godhead shuffle by him at the groan,
And beat him at the tunnel, to the street.

And leave to him the darkness of the cloud
Each bomber wrought, to prove that life was vain,
His heart, a tiny echo of the sound
Their dull explosions patterned at his brain.

Until he turned in panic, at the tide
And breeched, before the nurse could stem the flood
To kick his way in terror at the slide,
And cringe in silence, smeared with foetal blood.

While circled by a thousand crystal fires
He lay awhile, pretending to be dead,
But caught the acrid odour at his eyes,
And felt the windows splinter at his head.

The scent of fear had drowned the mother's smell,
And then the rubber, at the Mickey mask
Some torturer had long designed to spell
And catch his breath, and turn his mouth to ash.

And years that fled still saw him move in fear
On any street that threatened to confine,
He kept his silence strictly, by the year,
And breathed his air, and sought his own define.

While 'who' and 'why' and 'what' he read as lies
To twist and chart some long-term disarray,
To set the furrowed frown behind the eyes
That caught the mother, fretful at the clay.

That saw the father age beyond his years
And stoop, and grey, and crumble at his dust,
Before the woman's iron glance of love
Could humble, with her every tradesman's lust.

While he would play each rubbled hole that sank
Its memories in one explosive burst,
And catch his breath in shelters, dark and rank
Where he could tilt at shadows of his dearth.

And so he grew, and caught the early hope
That given time, he might explain his need
To drive each explanation from his mind
Before the questions drove him from his creed.

But dark suspicion brooded at each lie
And paralysed his will to move ahead,
He sought a deeper shadow at the thigh
To tempt from some unlovely wanton's bed.

Where he might coven, safe within her kind,
The darkness mask his fear before the breech
That sent him panicked, at some shrapnel rhyme
To burrow at the sigh, and taste the heat.

And lend him to another's frantic need
To feel some other flesh against her kind,
While he would wheel, and turn within his creed
To catch some distant echoes in his mind.

Bur search as ever searched, there's not a key
To tempt from time the secrets of that room,
Where distant shades of faded memory
Would drift, unbidden, at my mother's womb.

Bleak northern skies, you lost me at the spell
I carried since I spent my rabid wail,
I dredged my answers at your turbid well
In some attempt to grieve my tarnished grail.

But now I wait each bomb that breached the womb
To rain its horror, stain your crystal fires,
To end whatever need I ever felt
To answer for your self-lit funeral pyres.

14 November 1982

Blake

By field and by coppice
By tumbleweed and marigold,
Skipping at the butterflies
And chattering at the wood,
It's a handful of happiness
With chubby knees and tatters all
That scurried on to Christmas
Where the old grey man stood.

With a starfish in his buttonhole
And a penny wish for the wishing well
He romps home with a puppy dog
And a flower by his ear,
While the old grey man, smiling
Says: 'Mummy waits, in a little while -'
And I have a little whisper:
'I love you, my dear!'

23 November 1982

-1983-

Old Shades

High cliffs and rock pools,
The short sand
Where shadows lie,
The ice sea, the dark clouds
Lie long at
The inner eye.

What times pass between us,
What heart's break
At night's fall,
When old shades creep on us
To squeeze tears
From old gall.

And these days we sigh at
As love turns
To back away,
May stir scenes to cry at,
This grey head
Some long day.

22 January 1983

By Miner's Hands

What miner's art
Did meld and make,
Did stone on stone
Fling you on high,
Or lie beneath
The stars, awake
To think your shape
As nights sped by?

What weary hand
Did knead and tread
Your mud in some
Dead winter's storm,
While autumn's bride
Long kept her bed
To wait his will
Who gave you form.

And though they lie
Unknown at last,
Without foundation
Still you stand,
Your walls have stood
Six score of years
While they ran through
Their shift of sand!

And every furrow
At some brow
Did trace in mud
These barren lands,

Each humble cottage
Built in need
Was raised in pride
By miner's hands!

18 February 1983

Chimneys of Lime

I've walked at your ruins
To seek out your history,
Charted the runes of you
Stone upon stone,
I'm left with damp walls
And a sense of some mystery;
What tamed the pride
That led on to your fall?

Some spirit entangled you
Lived in you yesterday,
Drove you, dispersed, and then
Lay you down still,
Now all that is left
Is grim ruin and disarray,
Relics of life,
Strength of purpose, and will.

Cairns and old bones at
The granite-hard cemetery,
Mounds where no markers
Recall you to name,
Time has dispensed with
All need for your mimicry,

Art has replaced what
We thought to reclaim.

Each one that wonders will
Carry the seeds of you,
Sense all the needs of you
Time upon time,
And walk the sad ruins
That long life will lead us to,
Crumble tall hopes
Like your chimneys of lime.

In search of some answer
I tap your foundations,
I sound each stone wall that
Encapsulates time,
Your dearth and your downfall
Exceed your dimensions,
I walk at your ruins,
Tread softly your rhyme.

13 March 1983

An Old Coast

There's an old coast, an old coast
Bound by a wild sea,
Where I found myself, but travelled lost
For a year in every three;
Bitter the winds that blow the coast
For a year in every three!

The skies and cliffs are iron grey
And the gulls are blind in flight,
There isn't a way from the old coast
To be found by the moon's light,
When you're caught in need at the old coast
And the moon is dearth's delight.

I travelled north, I travelled south
In search of a friendly face,
But never an eye would look on me,
Nor check my troubled pace;
Lonely it was, and grim at mouth
I drift my measured trace.

I swore I'd leave that old coast
To look for the way I'd been,
The sea was still and the air was chill,
No roads lay in-between;
Time and again I found no sign
Of the man that I might have been.

So if you should come to an old coast
Bound by a wild sea,
Where never an eye will look on you
For a year in every three,
There's nothing to find but loneliness
And the storms that rage in me!

26 March 1983

To Keep My Wanton...

I, my friend
Who long have lost
A host of heaven
With every storm,
Would mar or mend
Despite the cost,
And carry all
I love to harm.

While age takes,
Breaks and bends me,
Rakes and wounds
Each tissue, tearing,
Only the hope
Of death mends me,
Grieves the flesh
Its long wearing.

Life bleeds
And goes before me
Leading pain
At every turning,
Only the need
Of love gnaws me,
Lending blame
To a soft yearning.

I, my friend
Who long have lost
A host of heaven
At every storm
Would gladly spend

Each word it cost
To keep my wanton
Woman warm.

29 March 1983

From Line to Grid

What day is ours?
What shadows paint
Their times on us
From germ to seed,
Each word that sparks
The minds of us
May inch us, years
Beyond our creed.

Then may we move
Far from the web
They wove us through,
Or we may dream;
Of painting stars
To crawl us through,
With little thought
Of what they mean.

While every year
Doles out the thread
That we may spend
Though not perceive,
We hope that every
Hurt will mend

Before it comes
Our turn to grieve.

As we have stepped
From line to grid
To feel each one
The way for him,
Long years have left
Our times undone
To pick us and
Our pockets clean.

12-13 June 1983

Tinder-Box

(Letter, 26 June 1983 from C.H. – 'By the time that I add my sign to this page the pallid sunlight will have dragged behind the Tree of Birds and spilled long shadows on my lawn.')

You, who sit beneath your tree of birds
To meld your muse, turn water into wine,
Have endless summers stored against their loss
That you might call
Delighted, into words
Before their fruit has wasted at the vine.

You tame your stars, cull every flickered spark
Like glimpses, struck from some old tinder-box
Of what should be, of some essential truth
That you have intercepted
At the arc
Of lightning, gleaned from storms and summer phlox.

And through your words, discernment is distilled
In me, to run me ragged at the dawn
Expressing thoughts you sparked in reverie
Beneath your birds,
Within the earth you tilled
That I might spill long shadows at your lawn.

29 June 1983

Dinosaurs

At what lame moment
Did our reason slip,
To leave us march forever
Lost at the cause,
With all that sullen certainty
Our catalyst,
To crust our blood, red-rim us,
Dinosaurs.

All force dissolves! All future impulse
Drags at our chain,
While others leap and gyre
Where we would tread,
So long disused, encrusted now
With crippled minds,
We only walk where, in the past
We bled!

When did the spark
Become the hated cliché?
When did 'we will'
Become the battered past;

It must have been when all eyes turned
To count the gains
That laurels fell, and turned to dust
At last!

18 July 1983

From A Blue Cloud

From a blue cloud at the two o'clock
And out of the rain,
With a long step and a swift nod
The master came.

Swinging behind him a painted box
In an old and tattered bag,
He watched my eye on the mystery box
And sat on a damson rag.

Under the pleat of his purple cloak
Was the Queen of petty spades,
'We're off to the end of the rainbow, Jack
To the long, black end of days!'

Ducking the light of the morning star
We hid in a tulip bed,
But caught the beam in a bottle-jar
To light the way ahead.

The master took some tinsel foil
To shake on the fairy phlox,
He said: 'You can have the Queen of Spades
Or the painted mystery box.'

I chose the Queen, who dredged a pit
To place the box within,
He tipped his hat with a weary nod,
'I'm on my way again!'

Now often I notice the Queen of Spades
Look long and long at me,
With a sad smile, she whispers on:
'Oh what, and what might we?'

While I still watch for the blue cloud
And the two o'clock bus,
In hopes that he and the mystery box....
He never does!

12 September 1983

Moon-Wake

One heart's ache ended,
Same as begun,
You had your way again,
Now there is one!
Gone as rent lightning
That darts at the eye,
Not one word mended
Nor even - 'Goodbye!'

Where now love's token?
Some sordid spill
Has left your dregs open
To whom may you will.

Caught in your moon-wake
As ever you do,
I'm left long heartache -
A head full of you!

8 November 1983

Spill Your Tears

You never knew I loved
'Til you had left,
And even then
You thought I was unkind,
Your moods had long
Distorted your vignette,
'Til I could fathom nothing
Of your mind!

And though your whims would feed
Your discontent,
And nothing seemed of worth
To make you stay,
I hoped that in the end
You would relent,
Accept the love that
You had cast away.

For love it was; and all
I had to give,
More precious than the gifts
That would delight,
Against the care that you

Would not believe,
All things decay, fall silent
In its sight!

And though you feel that
Love's about belief,
Each word of love is worth
A thousand deeds,
A word of love may cure
A year of grief,
A touch may serve the sum
Of all our needs.

I thought I'd overcome
The evil star
That patterned you to seek
My every fault,
That turned your every sentence
To a scar,
And locked what love you had
Deep in some vault.

But though your anger rages
At the thought
That love may well have been
Within your reach,
You chose to be a martyr
To your court,
To cry to order,
Once our love was breached!

And you alone have spurned
The only chance,

That lovers have
To put away the hurt,
Each word you wear like venom
On some lance,
And spill your tears for others,
At your skirt!

8 November 1983

On Receiving Your Letter for my 39th Grief

This poet grows grey-bearded,
Claws eyes, shuts out Seasons,
Love tales, reasons –
Lies, all lies!

Some long ague descends me
No word mends me
No sword spends me,
No love grieves me!

Lost as ever lost, I eat
My gruel,
And think of death
The tool of reason!

This long year
The black crow flies,
And takes my heart,
My head, my eyes
Beyond this season.

If I could start again…
No poet I, no pen!
No hopes, no dreams
All unfulfilled
No ragged expectations;
The hard cold light
Of truth would freeze
My lips, my eyes, my fingertips
And bond no lesion.

But now I feel the loved on keen
And pare the flesh,
While loss howls naked at the rib
And night descends
To snare my grief in…

23 November 1983

-1984-

Audition

Life, a Play
In three parts, now
Is two parts done.

In this,
The final interval
We rearrange our scores,
The Orchestra, still poised
Will sit
To practice discords
At the pit.

Then like rent cloth
The curtains start,
The stage is lit;
And I would venture
At my part...

Were I not so
Afraid of it.

24 January 1984

Pengellen

Each winter the grey-greying streets of Pengellen
Fall silent as dampness creeps in at the hearth,
And miners and men speak in whispers of heaven,
Of darkness and penance, of copper and dearth.

No children are seen on the streets of Pengellen,
Each wife fears her shadow, and hurries inside,
While mirrors have long been discarded, forgotten
That no man may see what his God may decide.

For so it was once that the men of Pengellen
Were busy and purposeful, masters of time,
The wealth that they won taught that greed was forgiven
Though every man feared, and was ruled by, the mine.

For deep in the earth with a pick or a chisel,
A shovel, an oath in a gaelic discourse,
They quarried the bowels of some God-awful midden
To pile the green copper in place of the gorse.

So pitted the surface from shaft to Pengellen,
So pitted and scorched that no flower would grow,
And brown was the landscape, and scarred was the bracken
That burst from the copper-green dirt down below.

While every stone cottage gleamed white in Pengellen
To mock at the bracken that patently lied,
For every small child played as happy as heaven
As if they believed they had God on their side.

The copper ran deeper than deep flowing runnels,
The miners would blast, and then pump and shore up,
'Til some had remarked, 'were the heavens so tunnelled
The mine would arrive with the first taken up.'

And higher and high were the skimps by Pengellen
'Like mountains by men' was the miner's assent,
Their pride went in hand with their wealth and their women,
And Godless and grim was the worship they spent.

They drilled to the sixty and six hundredth level,
With six levels more to blast out, pump and shore,
No man could have known that the deeper he tunnels,
The darker the horror he finds at his door.

They ranged at the back as the copper was falling,
Stood silent in shock at some evil refrain,
As into the light groped the Prince of the Morning
From where he'd been cast in his thousand year chain.

The miners streamed back to the streets of Pengellen,
They crowded the Kirk that had never been filled,
And prayed to the Lord they had always forsaken,
Then went to their cottages, locked themselves in.

While stamping and raging the length of Pengellen
He called for an anvil to shatter his chain,
The mist and ill wind that had told of his coming
Were never to lift from Pengellen again.

These sixty long years have brought change to Pengellen
No child has grown old and no miner has died,
They fast on a bread that is flat and unleavened,
And drink brackish water for penance beside.

The cottages now are both damp and rat-ridden,
Are grey and neglected, and empty of cheer,
And deep-dense the mist that encloses the midden
Pengellen is lost for the best of each year.

While whispered at evens are long supplications
White-faced behind windows both bolted and barred,
And dearth is a thousand years waiting to happen,
While green is a colour considered ill starr'd.

29 February 1984

For A Social Worker

What spark in you
Is this that burns
To comfort one
Whose well is pain,
That turns the nightmare
End of dreams
To thoughts of worth
From where they came?

And what the essence
Of your creed
That parts the cloud
In every stare,
You spend your lightning,
Spill each need
Then dredge and heal
Each long despair.

While at the mortgaged
End of dearth
They steal your essence,
Bleed your will,
To leave you sworn
To tears or mirth
While those who care...
Care for you still.

12 April 1984

Catherine Gables

What would you with me
Catherine Gables,
Turn my face
From my winter stables,
Call at the year
That my no-love lies in,
Treat the hurt
And the waste you're wise in,
Tease me and taunt
At the old love fables...
What would you with me,
Catherine Gables?

All of my shores
Are the grey of breakers
Seen from the tors of
Those same home-acres,
If there were time

And the old spark in me
I'd take heart
And a heart would win me,
Love was a dream
That I let slip past me;
What would you now,
Would you still unmask me?

If I could halt
At the port, no storm in
Red sky lit
At some shepherd's warning,
Maybe I'd take all the grief
That grieves me,
Bury it deep in the land
That needs me,
Bar the shutters
And bolt the stables,
Do what I would
With Catherine Gables!

10 June 1984

Twenty Years Down - (The Beatles)

All you left were your plastic pieces
Cloaked in covers of light and sound,
Whatever happened to spill our leases,
Wreck our passage and check our treaties
Twenty years down?

Often I've thought of the way you made it
Poked your tongues at the hand-me-downs,
Sang your songs of the maid, and laid it
Track on track, and the way you played it
Close to the ground.

And we all laughed at your small perfection
Simple lads in a world of wine,
We caught the spell of your sweet confections,
Song on song of your funny mentions
Of you, of me and mine.

The world was well that you had your way in,
Nobody hurt, or suffered or lost,
Nothing we thought that we had no say in,
Love was the word that we thought to play in
That took no count of the cost.

But now your shadows lie dim within us
And every laugh has a shattered sound,
Left to the rest of our lives, we spin us
Ever the wake of the dream that in us
Ran aground!

12 June 1984

Spoils Of War

I have sought our scattered scenes
In the seasons of the sun,
I have traced our wayward maps to find
Where we became undone,
Where the tattered snapshot tears
Spilling all we tried to hold,
What became of you, my lovely,
With your hair of yellow-gold?

For I only blinked an eye
Only seemed to pause, and then
You'd been lost to me for years and you
Were coming back again,
I have sat the night alone,
Sat the night to blink and stare,
I'll be old and grey, forgotten
When you're coming up for air.

And I've counted all the days
Though I can't remember one,
Since we went our different ways and let
Our tears dry in the sun,
I have caught your echoes blind
Like the man who never saw,
But you come back to me often, like
Some ancient spoil of war!

And I wonder where it lies,
Every year's repository,
Since the mirrors we once turned to
Ceased to look like you and me,

Though I turned to feed the spark
From the shadow of each lie,
You had slipped so far from me, I found
No trace of you and I.

I'm your father, as before,
You're my sweet, my spoils of war,
And I live with every memory
I garnered in my store.
You may think my love was lost,
That I left you far behind,
But I kept you with me always
In the forefront of my mind!

18 August 1984

Mother of Sons

The great themes are ended,
Too well and soon,
Not one I mended me
All in my afternoon.

I lay once conjured
In love where she lay,
All thoughts of causes then
Slipped them away.

Crabgrass and thistletop
Is all I have left me;
Not so, she comes now,
My woman, she mends me.

Faithful, she steals from
The web of my weavings,
Back-lit at dusklight
She picks at my leavings.

Storms at my tempests
And laps at my waters,
My mother of sons,
My dear lover of daughters.

Walks with me gently now
All in the night's cold
That I may be with her still,
When we grow old!

12 November 1984

Does She Stalk Pathways...

'How much we change...
I well remember when,'
She said --
But that was years before
And now, she's dead!

Who was she - why,
And what to me,
Who once lived, died,
Yet stirs my memory?

A brief spark, struck
From some ancient flint
That caught, soared, burned
Cooled,
Teetered at the brink;

Then sputtered, died
Leaving no mark,
No trail beyond the heavens
That sped her... Dark!

Her flight was short, sharp
Exquisite and pale,
Translucent, futile
She spilt her grail

With every seed spawned
At harvest's spring,
Her womb wide
She let them in.

All ruffians and whores
She bore to this,
The swift brief spark, struck
Then nothingness!

And why, when mirrors
Tell me I'm old,
Does she stalk pathways
I'd paved with gold?

10 December 1984

Spend and Grieve

Another year ended
Over and done,
What have we left of it
Now that it's gone
- What did we lend it?

Only the tears
Of the last year's spending,
Some of the fears
A beginning, some endings;
Raking our friends
By the pen and the sword with
No wound mending!

How at the fall of the next year, may
We garner our grievings;
Once we have plundered and purged at will
Our last year's leavings?

Only in time
May we learn our writ;
We spend and grieve
Befriend and leave –
So be it!

25 December 1984

-1985-

Tongues of Thorns

You think that I
Who broke your dream;
All that you lent
Was wasted there,
And I who spoke
In rhyme and scheme
Have lost the tongues
I tempted there.

You tear my shroud
Of wings and sighs
To leave me cold,
Unloved and lost,
While I live out
My storms and cries
In search of warmth
Beneath your dust.

But you stare long
At some surprise
That caught your glimpse
Beyond my door;
And the night's long,
And love bleeds,
While tongues of thorns
Rake my shore.

20 March 1985

Before We Part

And you, my father
Who cast my light
In the dim mists
At my mother's art –
The road narrows,
The pace speeds
And you may fall
Before we part.

Your threescore years
And ten are run,
And you must weary
At each stile
For somewhere soon
The stranger waits
In the long shades
By the dark mile.

And he will beckon
You with him
To leave us grieving
Every one,
No time to speak
Or bid goodbye
Just mute dismay
Once you are gone.

So should you wonder
As you turn
To glance behind
And leave us here;
We love you well –

This much you've won;
What else, you'll find
Will wait you there.

20 March 1985

Waters Into Wine

There is no love like the sea brings!
Of tides and storms, or your wanderings.
For you, too, swirl your eddies at the moon,
And flow and ebb at my every afternoon.

The mornings see you cold in discontent
Towing frostily at the night spent;
And gathering your gown around each rivulet
You scatter late stars in your bathroom pirouette.

But evenings - ah - and there the change begins,
When your warmer currents give my feelings wings,
And you lap at shores and forests ill-defined
'Til your breakers beat your waters into wine.

And when love casts long runnels at my feet
To swirl and charm, and make my life complete,
I glimpse beyond some hidden pool that lies
And fancy tides that move behind your eyes.

21 March 1985

I Work Machines

Some ride high pacers
Then buckle, then groom,
I toil the mornings
And weary by noon,
Some lie on beaches
While others sip wine,
I work my magic
From noon until nine.

Some pass each hour in
A long, speechless haze,
Some watch from windows
Some others, for days,
Some look for something
They cannot define,
I work machines
That decipher each line.

Some will learn nothing
Who sit by and wait
For life to approach them
Before it's too late,
I tend to secrets
In shape and in form,
Lending my essence
From dusk until dawn.

Others may wait
For the end of their spell,
I weave my magic
With engines from hell,
Engines of noise that

By dight and by dint
I coax from disaster
As slowly - they print!

25 March 1985

The Abbey

No longer knowing what or who I am
I turn,
This way and that for meaning,
Finding none,
But trapped within the body of a man
I know not.

The child I knew, and he remained supreme
Until
This beard turned grey,
The joints began to stiffen,
The dim reflections twisted to betray
One once thought lost to heaven.

Of all my time I have so little left,
And that exhausted, spent –
Squandered by him who thought
There was no cost in spending;
No giving up, no Lent.

From all to caul! Is this what we
Traverse,
Lost in our perversity and will,
Who spill our means, deny our source
Demean what knowledge shapes our course.

A shell remains, like some deserted Abbey;
And the gulls fly
Where monks once thought their spells,
And I....
I start at silences
Where long shadows, cowled, slink
Mutter at my carrells.

1 June 1985

Love Grows Slowly

You of the winter eye
Hoar frost and crab tree
Eyelids of ice, you lie
Beside and beyond me.

Cold are the storms of you
That scatter your needings,
Deep are the wells you fill
With other men's readings.

Leaving me wait for grace
And the autumn, its crowning,
Deep in the golden leaves
Here am I, drowning.

Playing that Patience, time...
That measures us only,
Whisper the one true line -
Love grows slowly.

3 June 1985

On My 2 Year Old, Leaving

Remember this, my son;
That when you left,
I had no hand in parting
You from me,
I had no wish to cause
More misery,
When you, in sleep's warm arms
Were wrenched from me!

Words are meaningless,
They die still-born,
Cold on the air, they shatter
At the touch,
When hearts refuse to listen
Over-much,
To what is said, or meant
Or left to trust!

And though you're gone, remember
What I've said,
That you're your father's son,
And always will –
I stand by all my children,
Every one,
And you may see me nights,
Stand by you still.

26 June 1985

It!

What did you mean
I'd 'learn from it?'
I learnt so much
That my spark was lit
When all that you spoke
Was holy writ
In the early years,
In the way of it.

I mused, and listened
And took it in,
And sought for the path
Of the way within
'Til I thought I'd found
Original sin –
And a box to tack
My religion in!

I cared so much
That my fingers bled,
My eyes ran blind
And my senses, dead!
My mind is numb
And my heart is bare –
Just what was the 'it'
In the 'that' out there?

27 June 1985

Do What You Will

'The best, you left with me!'
That part I loved in you
Is with me still,
And dream-sleeps in my memory –
Do what you will.

Nor will your storms and tempests
In their shallow pique
Drive it away.
Your moods and clamours melt
At my disarray.

To mutter at the distances
Long laid between us;
With sword and quill;
You cut me at the quick,
I score your spill.

'Til you do leave, have left,
Left me with this,
One battered heart;
I stroke and touch at will
Your better part!

While you play now at roaming
To mourn black birth,
In some deep glooming
At the dark side of the earth.

25 July 1985

Bitter Heart

And what strange time is this;
When all I loved has left,
And all I didn't
Crowds and breaches
My abyss!

With nothing left but silence
At my head,
They smile and murmur,
Claw and moan me
At my bed!

Where I can best forget
You ever were,
As buttocks, legs, thighs, lips
Deepen my despair.

For when I plunge and cry
And fall apart,
It's you I stab, and reach for,
Bitter Heart!

15 August 1985

One September Night

At one with me, this silence
Serves as death,
For no long sighs will ever
Catch at my breath.

Such times have gone, and rhythms
Subtly change,
Where love in me lay dying
Lies only pain.

For love itself, so weary now
Has tired of me,
Its darts lie shattered, spent
And lent, disastrously!

While I plod on, toward some
Unforgiving night,
Where dreams still tilt at shadows,
Try as they might!

9 September 1985

Once, When the World of Trees

A girl, not young
Is at my door beating,
'What do you want of me,'
A voice comes, speaking.

'Only of me and mine
That you took from me,
Only the comb and wine
That once belonged me.'

'I have no tines of yours,'
A voice is stating,
'Only the dark, these walls
A long time waiting.'

'What of that early breeze
That caught my blushing
Once, when the world of trees
Went by, rushing?'

'What of the glimpses caught
Of shadows, fleeting?
Open this dark, your door,
And speed our meeting.'

'Leave me to bury peace,'
A voice, it trembles
'I have no thought of lees,
Nor what resembles.'

'I have no window-panes
No frost, no hoar-dew,

Fingers that traced old stains
Were here before you.'

Bolting the shutters fast
I heard, despite me
Voices that spoke were mine,
Rasped deep inside me.

'Give me the breath,' she sobbed,
'That I once sighed with – '
'Never,' I said, 'that breath
Was the breath you lied with!'

8 December 1985

-1986-

On Leaving C.Y.S.S.
(The Community Youth Support Scheme)

Once more I mark
Another loss
Of things begun
I could not mend,
One more conclusion
Scrawled in blood
On pages I
Could not defend.

The many deaths
In life are these,

The small reverses,
Sad refrains,
We live with failure,
Ease our guilt
By seeking pathways
Fraught with pain.

But who would think
That I could leave
Without regrets
Is surely blind;
Our paths diverge -
Though I toil still
At the quarry face
Of humankind.

18 February 1986

Beached Morning

Steel grey above;
We tripped the silver beach
At some crisp, splintered morning
Traced beyond our line of reach,
We breathed the fluted air as if
In some remembrance
Of dreams once dreamed, let slip and tossed
Beyond deliverance.

And rivulets of cold did etch
Stark patterns in the sand,
While silence tugged at rock and pool
To spill their contraband;

I stole for you a morning shell
That caught the coloured sun,
But dreams and shells once dreamt and thieved
Mist over, every one.

The sea will lap the sandbar
The sand catch at the foot,
While we, so lost in wonder
Are as children, waking up.
The dream we live is lonely,
The plans we build – like sand,
The shell sparks at the sunlight
And I reach for your hand.

29 April 1986

Questing

And so, and so
And so must we
Trip at the brink – eternity!
Who shivers at this bleak abyss
As one moves forward,
So the next.

Down long, and down
And deep down went
'Til horses, men and torches spent,
One calls a halt to seek his lack
But on we travel – none turn back.
There is no way, for such as we
Go forward – back – eternally.

A hundred years at every step,
A thousand caught between each breath
As on we tread, the darkest deep
Man could imagine – caught in sleep.
No rest for us, though, tumbled years
Catch at our beards and turn to tears.

Nor can age weary, our decline
Is one of self outside of time.
Each journey is the same, and lies
By the deep pools, and the dark tides
Where the doubts live in their tall spires
To hide the truth from a world of liars.

For in us all are journeys yet
That we must take, before the fretted
Loose long web of time may spin
To turn outside us what was in;
To draw our darkness out from throats
That cry at night one long, high note.

And there is no way back for me
Who left my comrades, carelessly;
They seek the doubts I left unwritten
In a deep well, by a dark midden –
As deep, as dark as I would be
Did I not quest them endlessly.

15 June 1986

Well We Might

There once was time to sit and spin
The dream without, the light within
When young ideals like creed and rote
Would wreathe their blue tobacco smoke.

When wine was certain at each sip
When answers leapt at every lip,
Such were the days, when we all knew
If we were asked, what *we* would do.

But life began to call us in
And time, as such, has grown so thin,
We rush to do the things we must
While dreams, ideals, are things of dust.

And soon we turn our backs on them
Those shadows that were once young men
Who never dreamt hypocrisy
Would spill their dreams, philosophy;

And rule them with a rod of steel
And teach them well how not to feel,
And lead them blindly through their days –
They spare no thought for younger ways.

And where that dream, ideal, that once
Was held to spell deliverance?
Well we might ask, and well we might;
It's life, not death, puts out the light!

26 September 1986

-1987-

Old Pain

What now is my faded country
Since the waves have rolled me here,
Have cast me up on a stony beach
With the cold wind for cheer,
While everything I'd discarded
Was swept on the self-same tide,
The dross of an age's flotsam,
The dregs of an ancient pride.

The brink of an empty future
On the shores of a shattered past,
Where loss is the only teacher
And pain is the one repast,
The tall, old hopes of the morning
Dispersed with the morning mist,
The face, so brief at the window,
The child, now dispossessed!

I'll search old pain for my country
As the tide returns to the shore,
And beat on a past of anger,
Entreat at the loved one's door,
I'll gather my child about me
As he calls my name at the dawn,
We may yet play in the breakers
Of this life's long storm.

29 March 1987

Angel Head

Love is some trick
You play on me,
Some sleight, some glance,
Tenacity!
You tumble the sheets
At my marriage bed
And ride with me, desperately
Angel Head.

Caught at your eyes,
Your thighs, your touch,
I ramp at your sighs
Your cries – Enough!
Then drown in lips
That would raise me, dead,
And sleep at you breathlessly,
Angel Head.

17 April 1987

On the Death of My Father

My brain has turned to ash, and yes,
My mouth is dust,
And love is grief, and death is
But the loss of trust;
While life is paupered, futures turn,
Feed on the past,
And dwell on words you might have…
If I'd only asked!

No point to dwell again, but yet
I must, I will;
Was there some hint, a glimpse perhaps
You'd long distilled,
Was I so blind, insensible
And dead to grief
That death could snatch you carelessly,
Some petty thief?

Perspectives shift, horizons narrow,
Drift my sand,
Your loss has marked my end, that shallow
Sleight of man,
What now remains of you, I am
Though poor in creed,
For what you were was love, and this
I've lost indeed!

1 August 1987

Aftermath

We overplayed and underplayed our parts
And paid the price; we went our separate ways
For me to think of you, and you of me
Some part of all our long and restless days.
For what advantage? We may never know,
We cloud each other's vision at the hearth,
I loved you well, but love was not enough
We neither paused to give the other breath.

Like people trapped behind the moving screen
We both replay our scenes, we freeze each frame
Of shrugs, of nuance, words of lost intent
We blurted out in anger all the same.
But anger rests, and now there's only loss
As keen for me as you, I must confess
If I could still regain the way I came -
But mist and chill obscure our waywardness.

We charmed and chafed each other in our turn,
We stormed and raged, and whispered words of love,
And tried to use the magic we had known
To lighten hearts that long had ceased to move.
But at the end you left me in your pain
And I was too resigned to turn your head,
I'd fought and loved, and fought and loved in vain
'Til love was some black season I had bled.

What now for us, the doors are shut and barred,
The shutters strain at every passing gust,
And winter freezes over at the heart
To chill the brief young season of our lust.
We may yet meet at some pre-destined time
When life has buried both beneath its dross,
And I may look at you, and you at me
Without this deep and dreadful sense of loss.

23 August 1987

The Bloodletting

Each time you left,
Each one of you,
Each time that each one left;
To tear my rhyme and take my breath
With the sheer vindictive speed of you,
The mute, unfulfilled need of you
To do me death!

Your fury fed, fourfold, I said;
I bled in disbelief!
You packed my little ones, each one –
One of my little loved ones into your sad valise –
To twist the pain of your passing into
The stained-glass stains of your bloodletting
At the altar of my grief.

9 November 1987

Sink or Swim

The sea of storms came in
To batter our barley coast,
I was determined to sink or swim,
You to be drowned, and lost.
The lightning struck at our moorings,
The thunder silenced our needs,
The wind howled out our candles
And darkness caught at our creed.

But he was tossed in the fury,
Our love, our darling boy,
He clung to the drifting flotsam,
He clung to the well-loved toy.
One minute in every moment
Is lost to the best of men,
One moment of rage and anger
Cost me my lovely son.

The years went by in a whisper
A whisper of wind, and gone,
One moment, stark with lightning
Remains, while the stars shine on.
We touched for a parting moment,
We caught, touched fingers then leapt
Each to our storm forever;
- I reached for my son, and wept.

23 December 1987

-1988-

Theme for a New Daughter

You lie a-doze beneath a buttercup
That flowers at the cruel time of year,
To shine its yellow glow at cheek and lip
And celebrate your coming, at the hour.

While faeries trip, and leap, and dance abroad
Enchanted at each tiny fingertip,
They sprinkle stars to sparkle at each eye
And plant a crescent moon within each cheek.

While I, mere mortal man, will watch you pout
And smile and gurgle in your new content,
You crook your magic fingers at my dearth
And charm away the weary hours I've spent.

And work your new-found woman's wiles on me
Who should beware, or I may be undone,
What webs you weave, what spells, what sorcery;
My tiny witch, my faye… my Alison.

13 June 1988

Sonnet on Loss

You've gone again, and I sit granite faced,
Astare at this, the loss of my estate,
To count my grievings, seen as if afar
Through mist and hurt, and bramble patch and pain
Where life may only tear you at the briar,
To leave blood-blackberry patches at the stain
Of every love, turned ash, or died, or went
Beyond the realm of touch, or argument.
So here I sit, and never look aside
But stare ahead, pretending life pretence,
And sleep, that blessed anaesthetic state
As life, but turned about by accident –
While I, unmoved, unmoving sit in fear
That grief will overwhelm me as I stare.

31 October 1988

-1989-

Sanctuary

If I had time to think
I think
That you and you
Would loom immensely
At this dream;
This wrecked and wracked wrong-headed,
Foot-sliding, step-staggering brink;

This theme!

If I had time, and time
Took time for me,
I'd turn back twenty years
Of pain and doubt,
Undoubtedly;
And make my major moves
Before the long regret
In deep and tardy shifts
Left love, each one, one by one
In limbo - stranded yet.

And if I had you still, despite
My instability
Who loved me, as you love only;
Intense and bent to still my battered sanctuary;
At greener hills beyond my brink,

Then...would I lose you still,
When life's inept insanity
Tugged at my coat
And bid me - drink?

9 March 1989

Stalemate

I have no words, nor patterns left
To spill, my dear,
No facile quotes, no wisdom
To dispense,
Nor any careless answers at
My time of year
All that was lost, or sold,
Or buried, spent.

All gone; the well is dry, the depths
I tried to reach
Devoured me long before
I found you there,
I lent with empty gestures
What I thought to teach,
And questioned truth, if even truth
Could care.

So what is left; a feeling we
May not express,
While I doubt more and more
This arabesque,
That you find comfort now
More in my tardiness,
While I take heart at questions
You don't ask.

29 March 1989

Ship to Shore

When you pulled at the wheel with me
To steer our fragile ship of state
We nosed toward uncharted seas
But found our course within a lake.

And every where that we did turn
There loomed another barren shore,
We turned, and then did turn about
To find we'd sailed each course before.

And you would chafe at each restraint
And I would rush to catch each squall
That filled our sails a little while
Before we lay becalmed once more.

Then you would see each distant point
As bearings, where your freedom lay
And drive our ship before the storm
For day upon each battered day.

'Til we had sailed on every course
That wit or will could still devise
While biting tongue and sharp retort
Became the language of our lives.

At every turn, a shallow reef
To wreck the hopes that we had shared,
Each tack would bring us near to grief
Each luff would leave us near despair.

But then you spied some promised ground
And took the boat on that same shore
That we had left together, once
Though never to return, we swore.

The ship of state rolled drunkenly,
I could not steer, nor go ashore
And so each watched the other weep
For you would cry, and I implore.

'Til you rowed back to join the ship
But we were fast upon some reef,
And soon you turned to carp and wit
To speed you on your long retreat.

A thousand times you made that trip,
A thousand times from ship to shore
But now the tide's exposed the rip,
There's nothing left to journey for.

And you may live your life ashore
While I attend some new design,
Our ship of state once went to war -
I burned her to the waterline.

20 September 1989

-1990-

Where Once the Dreaming

As night it comes down feathered deep
I turn this way and that, to sleep;
I stare wide-eyed this moon of mine,
Bright pennied disc, on my face shine.

The every chill of generations
Clutches still this old heart's achings,
Turns all peace and warmth within me
Frost; and pale dismays begin me.

Loss of my own making, mine
Where once the dreaming brought bright wine,
But now each tear and old betrayal
Casts dark shadows at my fable.

Every cross-roads brings regret
As cheats and thieves may hang there yet;
But chains and fetters spill their prisons
Long before the moon its felons.

Such fools we are, who only listen
Once the moon's cold glance is given,
Cheap regrets and cold remarks
Are burned and scored on marble hearts.

21 July 1990

-1991-

Trench Warfare

From trench to trench
You followed me, to speed
My penance at the midnight hour of life,
Once all was lost, and mine the greater need
You came again, to gloat, and turn the knife.

It's always been the same
A thrust, then grief;
A few yards forward, then dig in, and damn the cost,
We worried at the borders of belief
To count advantage first, but never loss!

I can't remember peace,
There's never been
A time for me when war was not the game,
Each word a bullet, spat from lips that screamed;
You drank your deadly cocktails, then took aim.

'Til I was sorely wounded,
Sick at heart,
And pounded by the mortars of your mind;
I slept in foxholes, waking with a start
To seek relief in silence, marking time.

While tanks, like thunder
Rolled across my soul
To leave their shadow-tracks upon my brain,
My thoughts were camouflaged, and left untold,
And worked at night, while you explored your pain.

I lost my way, as if
I'd ever known
The forward from the back, the bleak terrain
That you and I once conquered, then disowned
Has left me not a landmark I could claim.

And so to this, the shadow
That at night
Will beckon me toward some ancient death,
When life has lost its paltry appetite
And I, the walking wounded, give it breath.

12 February 1991

Outlived

So this is your warren of secrets,
Old thoughts, in a bright new world;
How long did you think you'd keep it,
Before it was overturned?
We come, fresh-faced from the future
To bundle you into the past,
Along with the spells and sutures
Of a time, outlived at last.'

I turned to the young intruder
And paled at his discontent,
The arrogant eye unsmiling,
The lip curled in contempt.
'You think that the world's before you,'
I said to his youthful sneer,

'Well, I'll not keep or curb you,
Or your children will be here!'

14 June 1991

Never the God…

Your eyes bright, eager and trusting,
Where do we go from here, my son,
I spent my essence, loving and lusting,
Chasing a paper god, my son.

I turned my sword to a feathered quill,
Ensnared your mother's heart, my son,
She loved the god in the paper spill
But never the god in your father, son.

We came together when life was full
And loved at the morning light, my son,
'Til she grew heavy and I grew dull
While you just quickened and grew, my son.

Then you burst out like a single star
That beamed from our both horizons, son
We loved you more than the what-we-were
Than ever we loved each other, son.

So she grew bitter and sharp of tongue
And I went back to the pen, my son,
But all the words that I'd ever sung
Unravelled in desolation, son.

And when she left, she took you too,
The light in my life went out, my son,

I would she'd loved me as I loved you
But love is a laceration, son.

Now you have grown, the world's ahead,
Your eyes are eager and bright, my son;
Don't spend your essence on paper gods
Or trust in a woman's love, my son.

For dreams and all ambitions fade
When a woman leaves in a storm, my son,
Remember the price that your father paid;
Love sought and lost in a rhyme, my son.

13 September 1991

When Our Days Are Minutes...

At life's butt end, I offer this, my sweet,
A long, slow burn to, at last, defeat;
A dreamtime reverie of old, gone ways
And sleepy wakings at the nub of days.

A light touch, drowsy, on your fading skin
To feed slow warmth at your cold come-in,
A languid stroking at your liquid stirrings
Before sleep deepens and reclaims two virgins.

More long silences than words between us
(Thoughts drip silver where a word breeds fever),
Painful pauses at a mind's long ache
When a thought brings anger, or a word's too late.

All this, woman, can I see before us,
Life's long panic that will cut and draw us,
But still I'll hold you at the long-loved hand
When our days are minutes, and our minutes sand.

22 December 1991

-1992-

Dissolution...

The heart is still, there is no pounding at this beach,
The river runs its course toward the coast,
And life, once lived by two, is wrecked upon the breach
Where one may pass, but two are torn and lost.

Alone we came to this, and so, alone must leave,
Our slight conjunctions mark our passing days,
But there is more to partings than our hearts can grieve
And judgement dogs our steps, our wayward ways.

For as the river's lost within the pounding surf
So each of us are rolled into the sea,
Where less is more, and each is part of everything,
Alone again, but finally - and free!

2 February 1992

For Lyn

If I had loved them all, as I love you
Then life might not have been so much a waste,
For now, I find, it's all that I can do
To make the most of what I've left to taste.

My youth has gone, and all I hoped to be
Which makes you precious, more, and by the hour,
For when we're old, your scent will linger on
Like some long-faded, fragrant Spring-time flower.

27 May 1992

Condemned to Partings

We seem condemned to partings, you and I,
Whose love reached out and touched a world away,
I leapt at continents, and dreamed at sky,
And cried at night, that it should be this way!

But nothing jells, and we are still apart,
Brought down by others, phantoms from before,
If love could live in dreams, I'd take your heart
And fold it in my coat to keep you warm.

Then, dreams are foolish! We must meet the squalls
That tear the web of many an aching dream,
And forge ahead, and beat unfeeling walls,
For what, my love? For all that might have been!

And so do lovers lose, and so are torn,
And so does providence deny us peace,
The tears we shed are nothing to the storm
That rages at our head, and at our feet!

27 May 1992

Tablets of Jet

You think that you only
Weep in remembering,
Nothing I've told you
Would hint at regret,
But I have the candle
We burnt at our offerings,
That wreathed its despairings
On tablets of jet.

I wrote and I rhymed you
By sky and by water,
I loved and desired you
In metre and song,
But needs seem to blind you,
Enrage, and remind you
That love is one garment
You've never put on.

You lost us forever
Then bled at our wounding,
Cast back every metre
Of love I had penned;
But sent me sad couplets
Composed by dead poets

That brood on disasters
Like us – in the end.

Now my wound is deeper
And my wound is wider,
I live with it always
And always it bleeds;
For lines of my poems
Are stubbed in your ashtrays
And songs of your goings
Are burnt on my reeds.

3 June 1992

-1993-

In Ancient Time

And did those feet,
So bravely at the beach,
Set out determined, with the will to win,
Beside the cold blue sea that lapped,
That urged them on to greater strides, within.

I walked the shore
Behind these dual tracks,
To note their strides, the vigour shown in each,
They left such deep-drawn prints in sand,
When life was new - an endless stretch of beach!

The sun rose high,
Then soon began to dip,
Their prints diverged as his would tempt the sea,
Her smaller steps walked safer, at the side,
And watched him turn, in uncertainty!

The daylight fled,
And still I followed on,
Self-sworn to see the end of this, their joust,
Her prints grew deeper, with a shortened stride,
While his lurched in, and back, and out.

Each patterned sole
Like some distinctive tread,
Now broken, windswept, trailed its own design,
I followed blind, to read the road they trod,
Would they diverge? Or seek some common line?

And then I saw them,
Trailing dismal back,
His head hung, beaten; her great with child,
They spoke no word, the tide came to defeat them;
They passed on by, and my illusion died!

4 April 1993

On My Mother's 80th

There are no answers to your questionings;
If eighty years have not revealed the truth,
Then how could I, this child of your imaginings
Begin to comprehend your loss of youth?

Perhaps you let it slip and lose all meaning
When time last yawned, and you did fall asleep?
Then youth took flight while you stayed still and dreaming
Within some sepia'd year you once did keep.

Wild eyed and worn, you always look about you
And wonder what dismay has brought to this,
The thread of age has tied and bound and caught you
And thoughts of death now tremble at your lip.

But yet, your youth may still be seen and found there
Way back beside an old Welsh village pit
Where long dead miners carol 'Men of Harlech',
And fresh young girls in neat white pinnies sit;

To wait the miners singing at the darkness,
To wait the steelmen, wandering from the shift,
Until your brothers chaff you in the moonlight
And you go in, sit by the hearth, and sleep.

There are no questions now that I can answer,
There are no harvests left for us to reap,
For youth is spent and wasted on a moment
And age is all that we have left to keep.

9 October 1993

-1994-

When the Welsh of Wales Go Home

There's a distant drift of tides
That pitch at your troubled stare
And songs of a deep Welsh valley
Howl out from your wild, grey hair;
Then you sit, bright-eyed at the moonlight,
And you cry, bright-eyed at dawn,
There is no rest for the weary
When the Welsh of Wales go home.

You ride that distant country
While your eyes are mad with grief,
And you search for the things you lost there
Or you search for a long dead thief;
I speak, but get no answer
I question, cajole, implore,
You nod with an ancient wisdom,
And wake at a cottage door.

You knock, but find it empty
The thatch lies thick on the floor,
The shutters are hanging open
The latch, long torn from the door,
The sounds of distant children
You sense in the wind and weeds;
All gone, as if in an instant,
All scattered, like burdock seeds.

All gone, the lives you left there
Were storms that passed in the trees,
A light on the far horizon
Is all you have left of these,
For soon, you'll go to my father,
Where he went, so bitter, so far,
And the Wales of the Welsh will claim you
At the last 'Nos da.'

2 May 1994

In Your Dark Slated Halls

When I am away
And you are there
Padding the dark corners
And the distant stair,
I carry you with me
As quietly you sit
Deep lost in some thought;
Am I part of it?

And a hundred miles
May lie in between,
But the sky is blue
And the grass is green,
And you in my heart
Will lift my despair;
In your dark slated halls,
Am I with you there?

18 May 1994

White Horses

We stare at the rocks and shoreline
As if time itself has fled,
For the sea once lapped at our laughter
When he would go on, ahead;
But the seasons change in the counting
And the laughter fades from the eye,
He went ahead at the parting
Caught up in his own bleak tide.

Your hair turned white in the mourning
Your songs all died in your throat,
Your eyes turned wild, and haunting
As I looked for some antidote;
But age crept up and caught you
In a season of sad neglect,
We sit at the shore in silence
And think of some deep regret.

For the waves roll in like thunder
And the foam now caps the crest
And your wild, white hair blows ever
And your eyes are dim, distressed;
I hold your hand in silence
In hopes that you'll speak of him,
But you take a breath, and mutter
"White horses are coming in!"

And over the heads of breakers
Where the foam breaks loose at the rip
I fancy the manes of horses

Are tossed at the breaker's tip;
And shoulders pound at the rollers
While hooves flash white in the tide
And your dim grey eyes reflect them,
As you cry at their foam-flecked ride.

White horses, caught at the breakers
With manes of wild, white hair
They run at the shallow waters
In the hopes that he'll be there,
Their eyes are dim at the mourning
As the rollers set them free,
You smile at the heads a-tossing:
"White horses – coming for me!"

28 November 1994

Maps and Charts

For part of your voyage, Captain
I was there at the helm with you,
So young, and the world had flowered,
I caught my breath at the view;
But you stood grim, determined
And saw what I could not see,
You spoke of the storms and tempests
That I had coming to me.

Your words took shape, exploded,
Then burst at my head and heart
Like shooting stars in the sunset,
Like embers, glowed in the dark,

I lost so much of their meaning,
Ignored so much that was said
Your thoughts flashed bright on the water
Then dimmed, went out – despaired.

You tugged at my understanding
Set course for the verities,
I stood for so long behind you
That you merged with the skies and seas,
The breeze snapped long at the mizzen
The spinnaker billowed and flared,
I questioned the ship's direction
But I doubt if you even heard.

We parted one brave morning
When I took a ship of my own,
Then you drove alone at the sunset
While I made sail to roam,
We'd each glimpse sights of the other
At sea, and in seaports new,
When we'd spark our flints together
As my understanding grew.

Then my storms and tempests claimed me
As you'd said they would at the start,
And sparks came back of your warnings
As I set my course by the stars,
And I tried to grasp your secrets
That had glimmered and glowed in vain,
But you'd set a course for the sunset
And never came back again.

So now in my darkened cabin
I pore over maps and charts
And I set each course for the helmsman

To look for your many parts,
I know that the journey shortens
As the planets wheel and turn,
And you wait for me at the sunset
Where our maps and charts are burned.

26 December 1994

-1996-

The Turncoat

Set me out forewarned
While the heather glistened,
Tramped the starbright road
While my lady listened,
Soldiers at the doors,
Muskets at the casement,
All Kilmarnock groaned,
Milady in the basement.

There the road to Ayr
There the road to Dumfries
Torn by here or there
Mauchline; there lay Humphries:
'Where's the Laird o' Fife?'
Pikemen swarm all over,
All the red stained coats
By Portsmouth, and by Dover.

'Take the road,' she said,
'Take it, I'll come after,
Find the Laird o' Fife,
Lead us back to laughter,
Tell them Scotland's sons
Have been led to slaughter,
Let them beat their drums
And save the old Laird's daughter.'

On to Auckinleck
While the moon shines brightly
Cumnock came and went,
The horse drops dead beside me;
Sleep I by the light,
Tramp by wood and water
Lonely, night by night
For the old Laird's daughter.

Eyes that gleamed like stars
Lips that would despair me,
Hands so soft and fair,
Heart that would not spare me
Sat at Marchburns stream
Met a man called Donald:
'The army's in some dream,
The Laird is at Kirconnel.'

One more night on foot
I found the army lying –
'Where's the Laird of Fife?'
'In grief, the Laird is dying!'
Then I saw his head
Bowed and grey and broken,

'A horseman brought the news,
And news has brought a token.'

He showed me where the brooch
Was stained with bitter blood there,
From where Milady lay
He'd took it from her throat there,
And there the clasp was broke
Just where the pike had thrust it,
Had entered at her throat
And there the blood had rust it.

Late, by Kirk and brae
These nights there have I wandered,
Each eve I sit and pray
For love so basely squandered;
I have worn the red,
Lain long in the heather,
Sought Milady's bed
And loved her as no other.

'Take the road,' she said,
But I had long betrayed her,
Left her with the dead,
With Humphries men dismayed her,
On some night as this
And where my love is lying
Death will come as bliss,
And red will stain my piping.

13 August 1996

-1997-

How the Eye Deceives

I walked to the back verandah
And stared at the midnight sky,
The moon, long gone, lay hidden
By the rainclouds, up on high,
The wind howled out in the treetops
Then grunted back through the eaves,
My mood was black as the midden,
I thought – "How the eye deceives."

You lay with your back towards me
As you'd often lain in the past
When the gods of war were stalking
And your eyes turned red, and flashed.
My life, like the earth, was turning
While all you could do was weep,
And the pit of misunderstanding
Lay there, where you fell asleep.

I'd read in your daily journal
Some thoughts of yours that bled,
And knew that my life was over
From the words I'd found in your head.
We flared, dashed flints at each other
That sparked, lit fear and doubt,
While the storm outside kept building
And the fire in the hearth went out.

At two, or three in the morning
I rose with a fevered moan,
I thought that the air might soothe me
So staggered outside, alone;
But there by the back verandah
The earth had split like a pea,
Our path tailed off to nothing
While a planet lay in our tree.

And there lay a pit of darkness
Like no-one had ever seen,
A silence deep and deadly
So quiet, it drew me in;
I almost lost my balance
To fall in the deadly pit
Where not a star had glimmered,
No God had ever lit.

You lay with your back towards me
In peace, asleep, in bliss,
While I crawled round on the carpet
And punched at the mantlepiece,
Then madly I raised the covers
And dropped them again, in dread,
I sat on the floor 'til morning…
The stars shone under our bed!

You woke with a gentle shudder
And rolled to face me then,
Reached out, and smiled at the morning
And said – "I love you," then;
I felt the world come together,
A gentle breath at the eaves,

The stars were back in the heavens;
I thought – 'How the eye deceives.'

15 July 1997

-1998-

Passenger from Childhood

There was a bright-eyed boy
That no-one knows,
Who stowed away in steerage once,
I hid him in my clothes,
He always travelled second-class
And braved each raging sea,
We travelled while the tide was high;
He came ashore with me.

And every train I ever caught
I saw him there,
Back in some third-class carriage
Or just open to the air,
I started leaving him behind
Or caught another train,
Got off at stations where, I knew,
I'd lose him in the rain.

But one day then, I noticed
He was lost to me,
I hadn't counted on his hurt,
Or that he might abandon me;

So now it's left to me to brood awhile,
While he stares back from mirrors now,
And very rarely smiles.

13 January 1998

Early Morning Call

I rose at this a.m. and caught the phone
Its brittle ring,
I picked it up, I held it to my ear!
The static on the line was like
Some ancient offering,
But deep and dark and empty, like desire!

And then your voice, it rang down from past ages
Snapped your name,
When like a whip it crackled through the line,
Your voice then conjured clearings where
The crow cawed at the dawn,
And rattled windows shuttered in my mind.

Your call was brief, then gone; but I sat still,
As still as stone,
For the wasteland of the past had filled my well,
Where the trees had dripped at dawn
While the clearing echoed 'Gone!'
And tears of crystal shattered where they fell.

There is nothing I can do, life has come and gone
And you
Keep your feelings locked in shackles and in chain,

But if you should call again
I'll be out, and wandering
On pathways new, where 'love' is just a name.

17 September 1998

On Your 48th

And so to you my sweet, it comes
The point at which, three quarters gone
Life trickles through our fingers
Like the sand,
In some sad, damaged hour-glass,
That runs ahead of man.

Months pass in days, and weeks in hours,
And how we age – like flowers that wilt in time;
Though beauty lies, not in unblemished skin,
But deep inside;
And character and grace shine at our eyes.

We rarely speak of love, as once we did
With hot breath steaming at the window panes,
And where we, breathless, rode along
The rim of our content,
We now seek quiet comfort in green lanes.

I love you still, and more than you would know,
Love walks beside me on the golden sand,
It makes my heart beat faster
When you smile,
And leaps like lightning, when you touch my hand.

2 October 1998

-1999-

The Book of Numbers

These cheque book eyes that peer on out
With fifty four long years in train
Would beg the question, steeped in doubt:
'Are balances brought home the same?'

Are books of columns kept somewhere
With costs and profits to each name,
Does some laborious clerk inscribe
Each fall from grace, each cry of pain?

And is there some huge reference book,
A million pages long that gives
A code to score each passing thought,
To digitize each man that lives?

A ten for love that long survives
Its primal urge, a minus four
For each divorce, and minus three
For every child brought down, of course.

And how would grief be costed out?
A point for every tear or sigh,
Or nine to cover hearts of lead
That freeze in pain, but cannot cry.

For hope, ambition, faith and need
Are these the same for every man,

Or do the rich regain the creed
While poor men spill their lives like sand.

These cheque book eyes that peer on out
With fifty four long years in train
Appraise the wreckage of my life:
'Are balances brought home the same?'

17 February 1999

Nostradamus

This is the year that the gods will play in
That man, with his pride, will most dismay in,
While storms will clash, and wolves will bay in.

This is the year when the violent waters
Bury the land, as the ancients taught us,
And surge at the throats of our sons and daughters.

This is the year of the comet's vapour
When the earth burns red in its trail of paper
While men pray long at the midnight taper.

This is the year that our lord will spurn us,
Cast adrift, as the devil turns us
Slow on the spit of his earth-bound purpose.

This is the year that we lose our way in,
The planet reels, and the people pray in;
This is the year that the gods will play in.

13 June 1999

The Water Tower

I sit and stare at this empty page,
The wind howls long at the winter eaves,
The cloud is heavy, and black with rage
As squalls dance in through the myrtle leaves.

While deep inside in the cottage gloom
My love lies weary, cocooned in dreams,
I hear her cry in the darkened room
Call out one name from a nightmare scene.

'Michelle,' she mutters, then groans aloud
I grit my teeth at the open door,
The wind it eddies in dust and leaves
And echoes long at the water tower.

'Michelle, Michelle,' it grumbles and groans,
'Michelle,' it whispers, then skips and howls;
My love rolls over in deepest sleep
While I keep watch through the early hours.

The storm comes in and the rain drives down,
Batters at windows and roof in vain,
The wires whine in a humming frown:
'Michelle, Michelle,' is its one refrain.

And tears roll at my weathered cheek
The clock chimes five at the early hour,
Michelle once crawled from her bed, asleep,
And went to climb at the water tower.

Her hair was black as a raven's coat
Her eyes set back in that tiny face,
Three winters long was her spell of dreams
Before she crept to that dreadful place.

Three winters long was our fairy child
Who lisped and chattered from heart to heart,
The cottage door had a faulty latch –
I'd always meant to replace that part.

But now, awake from her nest of dreams
I see my love at the open door,
I wait in hope, but her eyes are ice;
She's staring out at the water tower.

Then I look down, and the page is full,
I've scribbled the words of an ancient rhyme,
Over and over and over again –
'I'll fix the latch when I get the time.'

And she goes back to her bed to cry
While I sit frozen beside the door,
The latch still rattles, the door's ajar;
I've punched three holes in the water tower.

13 June 1999

No-Name the Cat

The cat and I stare at the room
No-name the cat, the cat and I,
She stares at me, I at the gloom
The house lies still as a vaulted tomb.

She sits and waits, No-name the cat,
Sits and waits for a sign from me
But I in the corner chair am sat
And make no sign for No-name the cat.

We're all alone, alone are we
No-name the cat, the cat and I
Only the two, No-name and me
Yet once in the past we numbered three.

Now on the floor, between us two
No-name the cat, and me, lies you.
Your eyes are staring, your cheek is slack,
Your tongue's thrust out and your face is blue.

The cat and I stare at the room
No-name the cat, the cat and I,
She stares at me, I at the gloom
The house lies still as a vaulted tomb.

30 June 1999

-2005-

One by One...

If I should disappear one sudden night,
Escape, take flight, cast off my chains
And venture out one final time
Into the darkening light,
To leave this sinking hulk behind
Mired fast in weeds, and shallow deeds
That never now may be undone;
Take heed, I pray, who loved me once –
Death takes us, one by one!

If once you speak, but never get reply,
Though my eyes stare, not having said goodbye
When all that moved me, once, has gone
To join in common history the fate of everyman...
Don't cry for me, for I am well content;
A life, lived, loved, and now made more complete
By ending thus, as everything must end.
No – save your tears for those I leave behind,
Grief is for the living, not the dead and blind!

And if you need some final words from me
To give you hope, some ultimate destiny,
As each one passes from this mortal stage, I say
'Have faith!' - as you, too, approach the end of days.
Be calm, accept, and we shall all be saved,
Just as the servant, taking back the keys of life

Confronts the Master he has served, in every faith,
And hears the words: 'My son, you've done us proud!'
Gives back the key, and takes from him the shroud.

5 June 2005

Into the Light - III

Here I am, sixty-one,
I thought the end would have come and gone!
But then a light seemed to beckon me
To trip through another's history.
When China called, I know not why
I saw new future's I'd never tried,
The way was clear, my life was spent
So I fetched up in the Orient,
With all the bustle, the pomp, the pride,
I picked up the pen that I'd put aside,
For black-haired girls feed my heart's content
And children like jewels are heaven sent;
Is this the future, I know it's right....
       Out of the darkness
           Into the light!

China

This land of ancients grows on me
Like a soft moss, damp-oozed in time,
Sad breezes churn each soul, unfree,
And sweep me over, like some tide.

Strange voices echo from dim pasts
Long littered with dead Mandarins
I hear, I understand them less
But feel their presence in old sins.

While grace and beauty walk each street
As daughters fan their coal-black hair
The future calls to them, at last
And the world waits, to meet them there.

25 October 2005

Where Are the Birds of Wenzhou, Bei Bei

'The skies are empty and grey at dawn,
They're empty and brown at noon,
Where are the birds of Wenzhou, Bei Bei
Deep in the afternoon?
Even at dusk when the air is still
Or the cool breath heaves from the sea,
I wait for the beat of wings then, Bei Bei
Rushing to comfort me.'

'The birds were once when the paddy fields
Ran down by the river tides,
When the sky was blue and the air was clean
And the trees reached up to the stars.
The birds were here when the skies were clear
No buildings blocked the view...'
'But where are the birds of Wenzhou, Bei Bei
Why have they gone from you?'

'They left when the smog came rolling in
And the insects died on the ground,
When the grass turned white and the acid rain
Caused all the trees to drown.
They left when the river turned yellow mud
And the fields died under the road,
When men built towers of thirty floors,
They left the town in droves.'

The skies are empty and grey at dawn,
They're empty and brown at noon.
'The birds of Wenzhou took their nests
And travelled to old Hangzhou.
They went to live by a wondrous lake
That tales will tell, is blue...'
'Where are the birds of Wenzhou, Bei Bei...
Have they forsaken you?'

8 November 2005

Black-Haired Girls

The black-haired girls are graceful, like gazelles,
Their haughty stares would strike a 'lao wai' blind,
As they cruise on through streets, where rubbish spills,
Ignoring all, the poverty, the slime.

In knee high boots and skirts that lift the thigh,
In leathers, black, and frills and pretty lace,
They swing their hips so slowly, to invite
The dreams of men, who marvel at each face.

The teeth so white and straight, the lips that curl
In condescending fashion at each gaze,
The one brow arched, as if to look on down
From some great height they fashion from each frown.

If Gods and Godesses have ever walked
This petty planet's poor and pitted earth,
Those Gods have gone, the Goddesses remain,
To haunt old men, who worship at their shrine.

10 December 2005

The Man in the Chinese Moon

Both Zhang and Tao, and Wang and Chen
They stare at the Chinese moon,
For the fifteenth day of the eighth month
They've waited and prayed at noon,
They've thought of the woman whose name is known
And written in script and rune,
They ponder her beauty and sinuous shape
As they stare at the round, full moon.

While on some hill, four girls sit still,
Their eyes raised clear to the sky,
They sigh and dream at a cold moonbeam
As they flush, turn red, and cry,
The book could tell them their future loves
But the book is held on high,
And even the children that wait to be born
Are written in ink that's dry.

The man in the Chinese Moon, Yue Lao,
Is known to them, every one,
He keeps the book under lock and key
Lists every daughter and son,
Writes every lover before they're born
Their partner, and every swoon,
Then beams and frowns as their wishes sound,
The Man in the Chinese Moon!

11 December 2005

Blue Mountain Coffee

I take my seat at the Golden Grove
And watch the waitress, Xu,
She's sweet and pert, and her shortened skirt
Shows off a dimple or two;
She brings the menu, a pretty smile,
I get to the "Wo xiang yao...."
But she shakes her head, before I've said
What I want, would like, or how!

She points to the meal I didn't want,
I crease my 'lao wai' brow,
"No no – Lan shan" is my one response,
"Lan shan kafei, niu nai..."
Do you have it? – this *is* a coffee shop?
All I want is a cup – that's wrong?'
She rolls her eyes, looks up to the skies
And mutters: 'Wo bu dong!'

I check my book, have I overlooked
Some word, some phrase – a tone?
'This is a 'Kafei Dian?' I say,
She brings me a chicken bone,
Immersed in water that they call soup,
I feel a sweat coming on,
I wave my hand, 'bu xing, bu xing,'
She mutters a 'Wo bu dong!'

Can you say 'Yes?' Can you say 'No?'
She shakes her head, 'Mei you!'
The sweat breaks out on my fevered brow,
'Ni ting dong ma,' I go.

She smiles so sweet, she shakes her head,
She never will understand.
"Ni lan shan kafei or not," I cry,
She mutters 'Ni man man kan!'

"That's it, I'm off," I shout out loud,
'Wo yiao zou le," I roar,
She follows my every move as I
Make tracks for the outer door,
I pause and turn as I reach the street
To see her standing - then:
"Zy jian!' I snort, but she smiles at me:
"Goodbye – Please come again!"

(Glossary: - Wo xiang yao – I would like
Lan shan – Blue Mountain   Kafei – coffee
Niu nai – milk   Wo bu dong – I don't understand
Kafei Dian – Coffee Shop
bu xing – you can't/don't/ do this to me
Mei you – nothing.
Ni ting dong ma – Can you understand?
Ni man man kan – take your time.
Wo yao zou le – I want to leave. Zy jian – Goodbye.)

18 December 2005

Dragons

In the year of the Jade Emperor,
In the time of the people's pain,
The sun was hot, the people groaned
The sky gave up no rain;
'The sky gave up no rain,' he said,
'The ground was dry as a bone,
There were no rivers or lakes to feed
The crops that the people owned.
The rice lay waste in the paddy fields,
The people ate bark and clay,
While on the shores of the Eastern Sea
Four dragons laughed and played.'

'These creatures, made of snake and claw,
Of horn, and fire and scale,
Looked down to see the people pray,
To hear the people wail,
So Black, and Yellow, Long and Pearl,
For these were the dragons' names,
Felt sad for the people's plight, and said,
'We must bring on the rain!'
Without the rain, the people die,
They are so poor and thin,
We needs must enter at Heaven's Gate
So He will intervene!'

They flew to the Jade Emperor
Who promised to send them rain,
But then sat back with his minstrel songs,
Forgot the people's pain.

For ten long days the dragons paused
To wait the darkening clouds,
But only saw the people cry,
Lay out their dead in shrouds.
'They laid their dead in shrouds,' he said,
'The lastborn to the first,
The dragons said, "He heeds us not,
Won't slake the people's thirst."'

The dragons flew to the Eastern Sea,
They knew it would bring them pain,
But to ease the hurt of the brown, dead earth
What else, but the soothing rain?
Now, dragons' care for man's despair,
His hopes, his joys, his tears,
They send their many blessings down,
Relieve the people's fears.
They flew on out to the Eastern Sea
Its waters so clear and deep,
They flung it up to the heavens high
That what they'd sow, they'd reap.'

Then down it came in a storm of rain
That fed the people's joy,
They laughed aloud at this water cloud
That the dragons had employed.
The moment the Jade Emperor
By the Sea God was informed,
He stamped and raged, and bellowed loud
That he would not be scorned!
He called his Generals and his troops,
To make the dragons' answer,
Then called the Mountain God to him
To lie on them forever!

Caught fast beneath a mountain each
The dragons still were glad,
They'd saved the people from their pain,
The price they paid was sad;
But not unbearable, they thought,
So Long, and Black and Yellow,
With Pearl, devised another plan
That they might ever follow.
They turned their tails to rivers wide
To flow across each valley,
From West to East, the Long, the Black,
The Pearl flows, and the Yellow.

Four dragons' once, that cared for man,
Four dragons' spread their tails,
They fed the crops that man might eat,
Might sing or dance, not wail;
The Heilongjiang is River Black,
The Dragon of the north,
And south of him, the Huanghe flows,
The Yellow Dragon's course;
The Yangtze is the Dragon Long,
The Changjiang, to the mouth,
While Pearl is now the Zhujiang,
The Dragon of the south.

23 December 2005

-2006-

Terra Cotta Warrior

You stand with all your comrades in the van,
Unflinching, you survey the sweep of time,
Your eyes are sharp and stare, the man ahead
Does likewise, and your forehead wears a frown.

In darkness you were cast, you now appear
So sudden in the light, the dawn's grey wash,
The light is harsh and bright this time of year
And soon your colours fade, then turn to ash.

But what alarm is this that breaks the spell
That Emperor Qin Shi Huang had caused to lie
Unbroken on your shoulders since he fell
And sought his bliss in heaven, on Mount Li.

What terrors brought his army to the light
Revealed the might of Qin to modern man,
The archers with their bows, when arrows sang,
The chariots and the horses in full flight.

While you, with weapon raised, prepare to march
Your armour, dirt ingrained two thousand years,
Is ready for the clash, the battle din,
The slash of sword, the whine, the thrust of spears.

So who are these, the strangers who now stare
Forever in their awe at your design?

A face familiar here, another there,
May just be from your son or daughter's line.

Be proud, Dou shi, you come at last to stand
Revealed, to prove the potter's ancient craft,
While time stands still for all who see you there
To wonder at the world, where once, he laughed.

2 February 2006 - Xi'an

Riding the Wenzhou Bus

They squeak and rattle, and jerk and pull
And throw you across the floor,
The double-deckers, the number 5's,
The 3's and the 64,
They come in colours of red and blue,
Of green, and in spattered mud,
They wait for no-one but bully on through,
If you get in their way – there's blood!

The seats are plastic and hard as nails,
The roof is but four feet high,
You scramble along on your knees at the back,
Unless you're a dwarf, or sly -
And climb the stairs to the upper deck
To slide in the slime, and cuss,
You need to be dressed in your army boots
When riding the Wenzhou Bus!

The brakes are shot, they rumble and howl
As they wheeze and groan to a halt,

The body sways, and the rust is foul,
And they buck like a playful colt;
The roar of the engines is petty assault,
But your ears get used to the din,
The gears grind at the stop, the start,
And as second and third slide in.

But for one and a half, or just two Kwai
You can ride 'til the day is done,
You can watch the girls in their stylish clothes
All hanging on straps, each one,
With bags and baggage and cases full,
Watch peasants, or someone's boss,
Togged out in rags or in business suits
While riding the Wenzhou Bus.

And through the murk of the window panes,
All scratched, and marked, and fogged,
The Chinese go on their friendly way,
The rest of the world unplugged,
The shops, the temples, the slums, the views
Of the parks and squares – like us!
We rattle on by for just two Kwai
When riding the Wenzhou Bus.

28 February 2006

Swan Song

Her hair was as black as a starling's tail,
Her cheeks as pale as a swan,
Her eyes, like two slim moonstones, glowed
And her mouth was the Holy Grail.
She'd played in the dirt of the village street
So long ago, so long...
She'd swum in the pools of the mountain stream,
But now, that girl had gone.

While I still rise with the early bird
To tend to my father's fields,
As the only son of an only son
I watched the woman leave.
She cried sweet tears as she said farewell
And vowed to come back, and soon,
But the village streets of a western town
Hold nothing for Ling Xiaodan.

The weeks went by, then the months and years
And I heard of her, here and there,
She was dressed in expensive clothes, I heard,
She was driving a shiny car;
She was seen at the Beijing Opera
By a man who worked at the door,
'She glided by like a Queen,' he said,
'As her dress trailed long on the floor.'

And her wai po, down in the village square
Would brag of her daughter's girl,

'She will snare some man with a million yuan,'
She said, 'not a farmer's son.
Go home to your fields and forget her now,
She's not for an also-ran!'
And laughed, as the tears sprang into my eyes
For the love of Ling Xiaodan.

She came back once to the village street
To her home, as ever we must,
But carefully held her dress up high
To avoid the rubbish and dust,
I stood at the side and she looked at me,
Then turned, looked quickly away,
For Ling Xiaodan and a farmer's son
Had nothing at all to say.

But I saw her once before she left,
Alone by the mountain stream,
Her eyes were sorrowful, in remorse,
Remembering how we'd been.
'I loved you once, as a child,' she said
'But the world is harsh, and grey...
We do what our fathers want us to,
And my father sent me away.'

I sat by her then, and held her hand,
Stroking her neck, and hair,
And kissed the cheek, so pale and wan,
And I cried in a deep despair..
'You must get on with your life,' she said,
'Get a wife and a baby son;
I leave tomorrow to see the man
That my father has met in town.'

I heard that she'd wed a businessman,
And cried in the quiet gloom,
My dream had died by the mountain stream,
On that day, in the afternoon.
She worked in a shop her husband owned,
So they said, but I never heard
'Til the body was brought back home again,
That the love of my life was dead.

It seemed that she'd sold her favours there
In the rear of a grimy store,
To any man with the change to spare
While her husband played Mah Jongg.
He'd gambled his fortune, and lost it all
While his wife kept the fool from jail
With what she earned with her hands and hair,
And a mouth like the Holy Grail.

But then, a man who was ill or mad
Put his grimy hands at her throat,
And squeezed the life from the darling neck
That I'd once both loved, and stroked.
They buried her up on the mountainside
By the stream, in sight of her home,
And from where I stand in the paddy fields
I can see her pale white stone.

She'd played in the dirt of the village street
So long ago, so long...
She'd swum in the pools of the mountain stream,
But now, that girl had gone.
I married a woman I barely knew
And she bore me a black-haired girl,

With eyes like two slim moonstones, and...
A mouth like the Holy Grail.

10 March 2006

Bibles

You brought your Bibles and printed tracts
To a land that God has no heaven in,
For Tao, Confucious and Buddha, here
Had prior claims to the hearts you'd win.

You think you're holding a secret key
To truths that nobody else has found,
But minds far greater than yours despaired,
And you just cover the same old ground.

And pride lies heavy before a fall,
And vanity masks any truths you see,
The book you cherish is short on facts,
But lives in hopes, through eternity.

While all its chapters are written in blood,
The Jews, the Arabs, the Irish fools,
The swarthy Spanish Inquisitor
Who tore the flesh that he'd save poor souls.

The Reformation of England's Church,
All done for the sake of Anne Boleyn,
While Cranmer, Lambert, and Thomas More
Paid with their lives for Henry's sin.

I have no doubt that my God is there,
And sees the world through a mist of tears,

For what we've made of his mighty plan
Should shame us all for a thousand years.

But if it's a vengeful God you seek
Who waits to punish, and bring us pain,
I know him not, for the God **I** know
Would love us all, as I love my son.

But such as you can be never told,
You're sure, so sure, and you're born again;
Be sure that you live this life, not scold,
Good works aren't done on your knees, my friend!

13 March 2006

I Can't Find a Doll with a Chinese Face!

I've watched your children, playing in the sand,
Pretty little girls with a yellow hair-band,
Cheeky little boys with their snub-nosed faces,
Kicking and a-tripping over dragging shoe-laces,
Little brown eyes, and stubby little hands,
They laugh and delight, these children of the Han.
So why do their Ma ma's buy them little dolls
With blond hair and blue eyes from western malls?

Kan kan woman if you can can see,
Look in the mirror at your rare beauty;
Who's got the hair that would steal men's glances,
Coal black and straight, that your face enhances,
High cheek-bones, and your almond eyes
Now look at your child, be proud, be wise,

Why make them think they're less than they are
Than a blond haired bimbo in a western bar?

Sons of the dragon, and little princesses,
Need to be loved, to be held – caresses!
They should be playing with a doll just like them
Not something borrowed from a Disney production,
Toss all the Barbies and the blue-eyed babies,
Revel in the glow of your eastern features,
I'm just a westerner, wandering the place,
But I can't find a doll with a Chinese face!

22 March 2006

The Blueshell Bar

From Monday through to Friday and,
For some, on the weekends too,
There's a constant round of students here
Attacking the Chinglish stew,
They sweat on the riddle of English tense,
Of gender, of verb and noun,
But Friday nights and their teachers here
Are ready to hit the town.

In old Wenzhou, Canadians,
The Poms and the Aussies rule,
New Zealanders with their flattened vowels,
And Yanks with their godamm drawl,
The Scots are there with the Sassenachs
Their vowels like treacle glue,
'If ye' dinna gae doun tae the Blueshell, man,
I'll nae hae a drink wi' you!'

For after a week of adjectives,
Blank faces and wo bu dongs,
They're ready to slip their traces, and
Retreat to the restaurants,
Their prepositions are shelved at last
With a proposition or two,
Then they all go down to the Blueshell Bar
Where it huddles off Wendi Lu.

From ten o'clock to the early hours
They scramble for space at the bar,
The music's played at a surly scream
Or drops to a sullen roar,
There's Chinese faces as well in there,
And girls with a shapely rear,
All perched on stools with the foreign fools
While swilling the local beer.

And down the back there's another room
Where the groups philosophise,
Over a 'Jack' or a Vodka, man,
They talk of their loves and lives,
And over the mumble of bleary talk
A voice rings out at the brink:
'The world is screwed, it's over man...
It's time for another drink!'

'It's time for another drink,' he says,
And slams a Tequila down,
A 'Jack', a Bacardi One-Five-One,
A bottle of old Tsing Dao,
'I loved her man, but I let her go...'

I hear as I hit the street,
And stagger home in the early hours...
'Are you coming back?'
'Next week!'

1 April 2006

Pu Tong Hua

English is simple, it flitters from the tongue,
It means what it says when all's said and done,
No matter how we say it, stress it or declaim,
In English it always means the same, same, same!

Chinese is difficult, your 'Pu Tong Hua',
Is drawn in little pictures that go back so-o-o far,
And every one's a concept, with no strict meanings
Making it impossible to delve your gleanings.

As often as I study, and try as I might,
I can't get your xiang xing's or qing qing's right.
There isn't any gender; there isn't any tense,
So how can your past, present, future, make sense?

Then when I've mastered some simple Chinese
You say: 'That's fine – but it's Wenzhou-nese,
Nobody in Guangzhou, Wuhan or Beijing
Would understand a pennyworth of what you're saying!'

Every city's dialect differs from the main,
Canton-ese, Shanghai-nese, nothing is the same.
Beijing has its Mandarin, the old 'Pu Tong Hua',
But it's not what you'll hear in a Wenzhou bar.

So don't look for sympathy with adjectives and pauses,
Proper nouns or pronouns, adverbial clauses,
Your cousin's not your brother, and a 'she's' not a 'him',
But how do I tell you in your old Mandarin?

4 April 2006

Tense, You Buggers, Tense!

If 'I CAN' can, it's done right away,
'I CAN' never can do it yesterday,
'I can see, I can do, I can hear, I can feel,
'I can go, I can stay, I can move, I can steal.'

If 'I COULD' ever could, then he'd do it last week
Because 'I COULD' and 'I DID' are best mates,
                                        (so to speak).
'I could see, I could do, I could hear, I could feel,
I could go, I could stay, I could move, I could steal.'

If 'I DID' ever did it, the deed has been done,
'I DID' never does it right now, old son.
'I did not - You did too - So I did, you can sue,
What I did, when I did it, I did it for you.'

If 'I WILL' or 'I WOULD' or 'I SHOULD' are your thing,
Then don't hold your breath, it'll happen next spring,
'I will go, I will come, I will be, I will see,
I would stay if I could, I should get home for tea.'

But if 'I HAVE DONE' ever comes raising his head
The time has now gone, and the battle is dead.

'I have seen, I have heard, I have said in the past
I have travelled the world, I have finished, at last.'

7 April 2006

Beautiful Flower

You are God's best-kept secret, Yao Li Rong,
Your smile lights up the dimmest, darkest day,
And in your eyes, there shines a love so strong
That men are shamed, and look the other way.

For men are shallow, falling at your feet,
Protest undying love, then look a-stare
To see some dark-eyed daughter in the street,
And think that heaven has moved, to your despair.

While you provide what life has left to give,
Though age approaches, nothing turns your head,
Your eyes are fixed on what the elders teach
That love endures, until that love is dead!

Until that love is dead, or walks away,
Your love is faithful, fixed on one alone,
But this was never seen as quite enough
By those, whose feet were always set to roam.

Your culture still dictates the way you live,
The way you cleave to thoughts he may return,
That you may once again fill up his skies,
His one horizon, once he's come back home.

In China, there's no heaven, and no hell,
Except the place the lonely woman walks,
Who, long betrayed, seeks only to dispel
Her sadness, and her dreadful sense of loss!

Forget the past, forget the wayward feet,
Look only to the future now, Li Rong,
The best is yet to come, your lover's fate
Will seek you out, before this life is done!

20 April 2006

Don't Let Me Die in China, Lord!

I had a fright the other night,
I dreamt that I was ill,
The Angels fluttered round my bed,
They said: 'Now you be still!'
My heart beat like a pounding drum,
The pain was like a sword,
I had one thought, and only one:
'Don't let me die in China, Lord!'

The vision would not let me be,
I saw the future clear,
The landlord breaking down the door
To find me lying there.
'The Lao Wai's gone, not paid the rent!'
He'd say in pu tong hua,
'We'd better call the embassy
They'll send around a car.'

The embassy refused the car,
They didn't want to show,
'He must belong to someone else,
He isn't ours, you know!'
The neighbours filed in through the door
To look the last on me,
And clear the flat of anything
Not quite nailed down, you see.

'He looks all right, now that he's dead,'
One mother told her son,
'Perhaps we should have talked to him,'
'- a little late now, Mum!
They say he studied pu tong hua
But never got it sussed,
We'll have to make the funeral
As if he's one of us.'

So later on that day they brought
The baskets full of flowers,
The big round silvery disks that shone
While they drew straws for hours,
For who would wail and cry for me
As I had no-one near,
So two wai po's in old black clothes
Said: 'Fifty kwai an hour!'
For fifty kwai they set their chant
And woke the neighborhood,
And no one said to keep it down,
The Chinese understood.
A funeral is a sacred thing
For Han or old Yang Wei,

They kept their vigil for three days,
Then said: 'Today's the day!'

At four o'clock that morning
In the stilly dark, forlorn,
They set up all their crackers
To erupt before the dawn,
They woke up all the neighbours
Who came down to see who wept,
While other Lao Wai's turned in bed,
Rolled over, cursed, and slept.

And then the band, it started up,
An old Han marching song,
The big bass drum beat out of time,
A little late for some;
A little early for all those
Who just had got to sleep,
I wasn't quite the flavour of
The neighborhood that week.

At six o'clock they marched away
All following the hearse,
A wooden cart pulled by four men,
I thought: 'Could things be worse?'
They marched along the highway
Disregarding life and limb,
The band it played along the way
A revolution hymn.

Then I awoke, (the pain had gone),
A-tremble, in a sweat,
I wasn't ready then, I knew,
For Buddha's belly yet!

And so I raised my eyes on high
To plead, entreat, implore:
If you would grant me just one wish:
'Don't let me die in China, Lord!'

21 May 2006

(Lao wai – foreigner; Yang wei – foreign devil;
pu tong hua – Mandarin).

The Crazy Lady of Jiao Ba Lu

Jiao Ba Lu is an ancient street,
The cobbles are overgrown,
A few mean dwellings still bar their doors
The others are falling down;
They say a woman who lives down there
Is three parts gone to the moon,
While children mutter a curse, or pray
When she stumbles out in the gloom.

For Gao Fang Fang has pure white hair
That blows like a ghost in the breeze,
Her eyes are wild, and she never smiles,
And she often falls to her knees;
She falls to her knees with a cry of pain
At visions *she* only sees,
And wails at night when the moon is bright,
Or shadows form through the trees.

Over the hearth of her meagre home
Is a picture of Mao Zedong,

And she is there in the picture too
A girl with an armband on,
A girl with the light of reforming zeal
That shines from her hard black eyes,
Her hair tucked under a forage cap
With the rest of 'The Helmsman's' lies.

D'eng Xiao Bei was her only love,
So young in those distant days,
But he was the son of a landlord who
Was threatened to mend his ways,
They took his land and his money too
And cast him out in the rain,
While D'eng Xiao Bei hid his head in sin,
And cried for his father's pain.

Then one dread day in the neighborhood
The Red Guards came in force,
So Gao Fang Fang put her armband on
But D'eng just hid in the house;
They dragged him out as a traitor then,
And put him up on the stage,
But D'eng Xiao Bei had nothing to say
To the Guards in their rabid rage.

They tied his arms, they made him kneel,
They beat him with sticks and a club,
'Your father, he was a landlord pig,
So you are a turtle's egg!'
They tied a sign on his chest that said:
'I love not the Chairman Mao!'
And tried to make him confess his sins;
They'd still be waiting now!

While others pelted with rocks and eggs
Fang Fang looked on with shame,
She'd loved Xiao Bei with a burning love,
But nothing was now the same,
Her comrades urged her to show her zeal
To punish the 'running dog',
So she took a breath, picked up a rock
To fling at her one true love.

The rock was sharp, bitter and hard
And tore one eye from its core,
D'eng stared at her with his one good eye
As his blood seeped out on the floor,
Gao Fang Fang gasped, then looked aghast
And paled at the thing she'd done,
Then watched him die as the others cried:
'Long life to Mao Zedong!'

Fang Fang went home like one deranged,
And flung the band from her wrist,
So soon, in front of the People's Court
She was termed a 'revisionist!'
For ten long years in a prison cell
She wept and cried: ' Enough!'
But the years did nothing to soothe the pain
Of killing her one true love.

And still she lives at Jiao Ba Lu,
Alone, in the dark she cries
In a part of town that's coming down,
Just like 'The Helmsman's' lies.
Those days have gone, but the lady wails

As she works away at the loom,
While the neighbours shake their heads and say:
'She's three parts gone to the moon!'

2 June, 2006

Chingl-ai

I have left my heart
In the high, high sky
That you might still see
When I'm gone, close by;
And I took your love
When you slept, sound, deep
And carried love away
Like a robber in your sleep.

I wrapped it in feathers
And put it in a sack,
Hid it in a forest, then
Carried on my back,
Took a peek at nightshine
Saw the feathers heave,
Heard a little sigh then:
'Why did you leave?'

And my tears flew wide
To the river, so long
That the banks ran over
'Til the people were gone,
I'm a one man only
Like a dark, dark star

While you sky light morning
With a face-cream jar.

I loved you then
Like I love you now
Like a heart that bursts
On an old ship's prow;
Though I had to leave
When the moon went round
I will love you forever
'Til the sun burns down.

19 June 2006

The Endless Taxi

I staggered out of the Monkey Ba
At three... or was it four?
I'd lost my watch and wallet there,
I'd not been there before,
But after drinks or three, I think
I wasn't seeing straight,
I only knew I'd smoked my last
So knew it must be late.

I searched my pockets, plumbed the depths
And found a crumpled note,
A twenty kwai had 'scaped my eye,
Thank god for kindly fate!
I had a choice of yi bao yan,
A pack of Xinanjiang,
Or I could grab a 'jiao che' home
At a cost of shi yuan!

I chose the smokes, and spent the ten,
That left me ten to go,
I knew the cost to Xia Lv Pu
Should only be ten kwai,
I hailed a Yellow Jiao Che and
Fell in the open door,
The cabbie grunted 'na li – ah',
I mumbled: 'Xia Lv Pu!'

My eyes were somewhat fuzzy
Rolling round my empty head,
I focused on the meter box,
Its numbers glowing red,
'Shi er', it said, or twelve yuan,
That's when I sobered up;
Of course! Midnight! - the fares increase,
I didn't have enough!

We got to Xia Lv Pu too soon,
I shook my weary head,
And muttered 'Ming Hang Lu, old chum,
Qu Ming Hang Lu,' instead;
The cabbie looked me up and down,
Then shrugged and turned about,
And back we went to Ming Hang Lu,
The meter jumped about.

At fifteen kwai we hit the Lu,
I muttered, 'Qu da Xue,'
'Cos that was where the campus was,
And where I'd find old Lou;
He'd surely loan me twenty kwai
To pay for the blasted car,

But then I realised... I'd left
Old Lou at the Monkey Ba.

I tapped the dash, and said: 'Hao de!
Wo yao qu Jiang Xing Island,
The cabbie was looking murderous,
I sensed that he wasn't smiling;
They've got no sense of humour here,
They're all just money crazy,
But still he turned and gunned the cab,
The meter was looking hazy.

By thirty kwai I'd lost the plot,
The Monkey Ba had closed,
Old Lou was nowhere to be seen,
I said: 'Wo qu Hangzhou!'
He muttered something like 'Shagua!
Ni shi bendan,' he said,
I flung the Xinanjiang at him,
Jumped out the cab, and fled!

So here I am, ten miles from home,
He's headed for 'gang ting',
I think my luck is running out,
The police will run me in.
I wouldn't mind, a place to sleep
Would do me, I won't fret,
The only thing that bugs me is
I've got no cigarettes!'

23 June 2006

(Glossary and pronunciation:
Ba – Bar. Twenty Kwai (Kwy) – 20 yuan
yi bao yan (ee bough yen) – one box cigarettes

Xinanjiang (See nan jang) – Brand of cigarettes
Jiao Che (Jou –as in ouch – Chuh) – Taxi
Shi yuan (Cher you ann) – 10 yuan.
Xia Lv Pu (She ah Luh Por)- a district in Wenzhou
na li – ah (narli-ah) where? The 'ah' is Wenzhounese.
shi er (Cher aahh) – twelve. Ming Hang Lu (Meen Haang Lou) – the name of a road. Qu – (chew) go to.
Qu da Xue (chew dar sure) – go to the University.
Hao de – (How luh) - Okay! Wo yao qu Jiang Xin – (Wore yow – as in ouch – chew Jang Sheen)
I want to go to Jiang Xin Island. Wo qu Hangzhou (Wore chew Hangzoe) – I want to go to Hangzhou – capital of Zhejiang Province, about 300 miles away. Shagua (Shag wa) – idiot!
Ni shi bendan (Knee sir ben dan) – You're foolish!
gang ting (Garng Ting) – the police station.)

Before I forget...

The China stint is over,
There's only a week to go,
I packed up a box of souvenirs
And trudged to the 'you zheng ju',
They cost me an arm and leg to send
By 'shui lu lu xin jian,'
I just have to pack a suitcase now,
Say 'ron' to a special friend.

The apartment's almost empty,
It looks quite bare, forlorn,
As bare as the heart I gave to them
The people of old Zhejiang,
Their lives will go on without me now
As I head to the 'Fei ji chang,'
But I take my memories, every one
To the land where I come from.

The children dancing at 'Dou Mei Li,'
At the end of Wendi Lu,
The neon signs, the disco bars
And the Chimp from the Wenzhou Zoo,
The rat-tat-chatter of Chinese girls
The smiles from a Chinese cop,
The crazy lady at Ming Hang Lu
At the 'I am your friend'-ly shop.

The buses rattling by non-stop
That take you to who knows where,
The moonlight rides in a trike, red top,
The crazies that drive 'Jiao Che's',
All this I'll remember while travelling home,
Then back to my life before,
But many a Chinese Moon will wane
Before I forget Zhong guo!

26 June 2006

(Glossary and Pronunciation:
you zheng ju (Yo jung jew) – the Post Office
Shui lu lu xin jian (Shway loo loo shin jen) – Surface Mail
ron – Aussie expression – 'Catch ya late(r on).
Zhejiang (Ger –as in Germany – jang) – A Chinese Province.
Fei ji chang (Fay gee chang) – airport.
Dou mei li (Doe may lee) – Do&Me – Chicken place like KFC
Wendi Lu (Wendy Loo) – Wendi Street.
Ming Hang Lu (Meen Haang Loo) – Ming Hang Street.
'I am your friend' is the one English phrase known by this lady.
Jiao Che (Jow – as in ouch – Tchur) – Taxi
Zhong guo (Jong gwor) – China.

The Beggar of Wu Ma Jie

He's laid his head on a Chinese street
There's nothing of dignity here,
He's bared his soul in a plastic bowl
For the rest of the world to jeer,
His clothes are ragged, his body is torn
With a million kinds of sin,
The sort that everyone walking past
Holds close; hides under the skin.

He lies in dirt on a filthy rag
To keep the cold from his bones,
And never utters a word to beg,
Though often he cries, or groans,
His face is one with the living earth
As he rests his head on the ground,
He's soaked by the chilling winter rains
And washed by the summer storms.

His bowl holds only a few yuan
That those with a humble heart
Might drop in shame, then hurry away
From a life that's fallen apart;
There's no compassion in passing eyes
Just the hint of a prideful sneer,
That damns us all to the final fall
As we taste of his deep despair.

Our Lord, or Buddha, in heat or cold
You lie in his wretched form,
To feel the toll of a human soul
Who's lost to his wife and home;

A man walks tall in the morning sun
Is crippled by those held dear,
Then falls to earth, is there no repair
For the beggar of Wu Ma Jie?

13 December 2006

(Wu Ma Jie – pronounced: Oo Ma Jeer).

-2007-

I Waste My Days….

In the half-twilight of my empty year
Where I crouch, hemmed in
By an avalanche of days,
I hear the trees murmur
In some long, sad fatigue,
While birds land, hover…
And break their journeys.

My life has bunched its folds,
They gather at my feet,
As clouds, grey, scud across each enterprise;
Behind my eyes are glimpses of
Lost days, more sure and wise,
While love lies, mocking me,
And each year cries…

The clock ticks relentlessly,
The dead leaves fall,

My lost friends walk at my horizons,
The things I found familiar
Have ceased to draw my gaze…
While death's sleep beckons me
I waste my days…

26 September 2007

A Pensioners Prayer

Good God Almighty,
What's to become of me?
Since I turned sixty
Nobody's wanted me,
Even my job
Disappeared at the company,
Forty five years -
Now they just dump me!

Friends have moved on
The children have grown,
Burdened with worries
And kids of their own,
All the ex-spouses
Have taken my Super
Along with the houses
And my Mini-Cooper.

I paid all my taxes
But now that I'm pensioned
The government thinks
That it's best I'm not mentioned.
They say if I'm quiet

And don't make a fuss,
They won't Euthanase/-
Push me under a bus!

They say that I'll get
My reward up in heaven,
But now I subsist on the
Pittance I'm given.
I'm worth less than scrap,
That's the truth, that's the sum of me,
Good God Almighty –
What's to become of me?

26 September, 2007

Why Does My Faith…

I sang in the choir when I was young,
In surplice, ruff, and gown,
I bent my head to the cherubim
And cast my eyes to the ground,
I read your word in the Holy Book
And swore to be good and true
While living in fear of an Awe-ful God,
A life spent, looking for you.

My mind was full of heaven and hell
And the things that I shouldn't do,
But the world seemed bent on a wayward course
All done in the name of You…
For 'Christ Almighty' I heard on lips
That shouldn't have breathed their sin,

And 'Jesus Christ' is a dirty word…
But why does my faith grow thin?

The world has turned to greed and lust,
To hate, to me for mine,
And life is cheap on the empty streets
Where drugs are the bottom line,
Where children murder their parents
And the parents murder their young,
Where everyone has a mobile phone
But none with your number on!

It's long since I tossed heaven and hell
To rot in a garbage bin
But still maintained my faith in you,
Your pain in an earthly skin;
I still believe in an afterlife,
And I know that you'll see us in,
I'm closer to you than I've ever been
So why does my faith grow thin?

24 October, 2007

Goddo & Me

'He slept through the Paleozoic Age,
He yawned through Neanderthal Man,
When dinosaurs walked, he was fixing a hole
In the floor of the Sea of Japan,
When Lincoln was making your favourite speech
He was out with a spanner, near Mars,
Adjusting some angle, inclined to the sun,
And admiring his favourite Stars.'

'It was fun in those days, when he used to display
An amazing addiction to Math,
His Geometry, angles, and parallel spangles
He'd scatter whilst running his bath;
His compass, divider and measuring tools
I would hide, with the keys to his locks,
When questioned, he'd say that he'd need them today
For precessing the Equinox.'

'I never thought much of mechanical things,
I left all that headwork to him,
I wanted some other distraction for me
So he gave me Original Sin;
He made me an Adam, then added an Eve
And he left me to play – (on my terms);
I sent them an Avatar Serpent to tempt,
And an apple, corrupted with worms.'

'He left me alone for a while, I suppose,
While adjusting Orion, its Belt,
For thousands of years I played havoc with those
Who thought Eve was spelt Evil – Misspelt!

The trouble began when he came back again
And he saw what I'd done to his art,
That stuff about tempting his son, I declare
It was innocent fun - Cross my heart!'

'Now lately he seems to be old, and he's tired
And he sleeps while the engine goes round,
When he wakes and he knuckles his rheumy old eyes,
I just tell him the planet is sound.
But cyclones and earthquakes and floodings and droughts
Are my special pet projects, you see;
I hate to be bored, and it's only good sport
For the likes of old Goddo and me!'

29 November 2007

To My Wives

You may believe, my ladies dear,
I took away your sun,
To cloak you in my darkness
While our time was left to run;
You may believe I took your youth
And brought you to despair,
But that was not my purpose;
It was life that took us there.

The old recriminations
That have saddened all my years,
As each and every one of you
Went off, in search of tears,
The old recriminations, using
Truths I can't retract,
Come back to haunt me, every one:
'Was I as bad as that?'

The life that is behind us now
Is locked in some old hearse,
You've moved along, and like the song
You sing another verse,
But I sit in the dark, and hear
Each word you brought, undone,
And swear before the living God:
'I loved you, every one!'

23 December 2007

Dong Tou Dao

I cannot stay, I cannot go,
And where I am but you would know,
I walk where feet have walked before
But your feet linger at the shore.

The sea, immense, this great divide
With each on each, the other side,
Where once we walked as moon on moon,
Now one must light our afternoon.

That narrow beach, I see it now,
That lonely beach at Dong Tou Dao
Where you laughed once, like tinkle bells
While I went looking for strange shells.

And when you walked, so full of grace
Along the sand, that lonely place
I saw my moon reflect your eyes
With ancient wisdom, speak Chinese.

A day I will remember when
All youth has rendered folk old men,
But you will young be, fair of face
At Dong Tou Beach, I see you pace.

And all I have that keeps me sane
Are moving images – each frame
Recalls that laughing girl, that day
Repeating, like some roundelay.

My past will not now let me go
As cold and chills me overflow,
I would I had not left you now…
I left my heart at Dong Tou Dao.

24 December 2007

(Pron. 'Dung Toe Dow')

Somebody Help!

The earth's beginning to creak and groan
Like a rusty hinge in a country home
Or an ancient voice on the telephone,
That screeches – 'Somebody help!'

Too many people, somebody said,
Too much carbon, not enough bread,
Too much greed in the neighborhood,
But please – 'Somebody help!'

Trees are burning, the fields are dry
The sun is scorching the southern sky,
The ice is melting, so by and by
Won't please – 'Somebody help!'

The earth is cracking from rim to rim
While water drains from the river's brim,
The smoke pours out 'til the light goes dim,
Stand up! – 'Somebody help!'

The rich get rich and the poor get poor
But nobody's worried except Al Gore,
I wonder what God in his wisdom saw –
'Won't somebody – Somebody Help!'

24 December 2007

China Song – (Zhōng guó gē qǔ)

Last night I heard a Chinese song
That conjured almond eyes,
It swelled and soared, and took the air
I sought to breathe, my friend,
That song poured out the sadness that
I'd seen behind your lies,
It soared and swelled, and slipped and dipped,
Heartbroken at the end.

But you just smiled and chattered,
Though your words were terse and bleak,
They hid some strange confusion, and
A hurt that would not mend,
I'd seen you cry before, with not
A tear on either cheek,
When Chinese tear-ducts dry, but cry -
It seems that you pretend.

Five thousand years of sorrow
Taught you Chinese not to weep,
To show no strong emotion, to
Accept the fate you're sent,
The pendulum that swings one way,

May cut you while you sleep,
But always swings the other way
Confucius say - my friend!

So all your love and laughter and
The sadness of your past,
Is built in to the music that your
Cultured songsters write,
And truly, when I listen
To that swelling sound at last,
Your tears well up, and overflow
From *my eyes*, every night.

26 December 2007

The Burglar Dog

I have a dog called Harry,
He's a Maltese-Poodle cross,
I don't know how I got him -
(He saw me coming! – Of course!)
The little rat sleeps on my couch
And scatters his bones about,
His hair's all over the washing pile
And I'm constantly kicking him out.

Then he goes for the doggy wounded look,
And lies in the sun, outside,
Rolls in the grass and the prickles, waits
For my temper to subside.
I say – 'Who spilt the rubbish, then,
All over the kitchen floor?'

He sniffs – 'It was the Burglar Dog.'
- Refuses to say any more.

The Burglar Dog, the Burglar Dog!
That's all that I ever hear,
Whenever my steak goes missing
It's the Burglar Dog, I fear.
He comes in the house while I'm in bed,
And Harry's asleep on the couch,
Opens my packet of crinkle chips
And sneaks them out of the house.

He comes and he chews my slippers up
While Harry's away, outside,
Performing his own ablutions
So he tells me - Bless my eyes!
Crapping all over the garden path
Where I walk, no doubt it's him!
'Not me – must be the Burglar Dog!
You must have let him in!'

I've never seen this Burglar Dog
But I'm going to lie in wait,
Set up my digital camera then,
And catch this dog in the act;
But if it happens to be pure white,
All fluffy and one foot tall,
Harry will have some explaining to do -
Or I'll take away his ball(s)!

25 December 2007

-2008-

Shoes

'Get rid of those old shoes,' she said,
'Their time has come and gone.'
I looked down at my battered soles
And smiled, as she went on;
When women talk of 'romance', then
It must be dressed to kill,
But these old shoes saw more romance
Than she could ever tell!

I took these shoes to China,
They passed through Singapore,
They trod old Wenzhou's meaner streets
In silence, pride and awe;
They padded through fine Restaurants
And stood before my class,
While Chinese students bit their pens
Translating Poe, en masse.

These shoes took me to Shanghai,
To walk the Nanjing Road,
They stood while shoppers gaily passed
And chattered some sweet code,
These shoes have trod through old Beijing
The Square, Tian'anmen,
Where Marco Polo did his thing
My shoes had followed on.

They walked the Summer Palace
Where Emperors played their roles,
A thousand years of history
Was scuffed beneath their soles,
They slithered over Kunming Lake
Long frozen, on the ice,
They strolled the Bronze Pavilion
Like some ancient paradise.

Then on the heights at Ba-da-ling
They helped me climb 'The Wall',
They dragged my poor old bones aloft,
I thought that I would fall,
They paced beside the Terra Cotta
Warriors at Xi'an,
These shoes have seen more romance
Than a new pair ever can.

'Get rid of these old shoes, my dear,
I couldn't, I regret;
I bought them when I first met you,
When we were young, my pet!
They hold too many memories
Of how we were back when;
I'll keep them underneath our bed - '
The wife - she kissed me then!

21 February 2008

Obit.

Jennifer Absalom Maudlin-Mand
Passed away yesterday, by her own hand,
Scribbled a note to be found once she'd done it,
'Please put the strawberries back in the punnet!
I am so weary of life and the living,
Tell all my friends, it's all right! I forgive them!'

Jennifer penned all her poetry passé,
Lolled all her life on the lawn, on the grassé,
Painted her pictures from life in the nuddy,
Rolled in the puddles and made herself muddy,
Nothing survives of her art or her passion,
Only stained clothes that she rolled in the grass on.

'Wealth is a burden!' was one of her utters,
'Time is so tedious!' 'Love is for nutters!'
'I am so jaded with cell phones and gadgets,
Emails and sea sails, and that poet, Paget,
I have done everything, been there and spent it,
Now I look forward, I'm planning to end it.'

Jennifer Absalom Maudlin-Mand
Passed away yesterday, by her own hand,
Stuck her two fingers inside a light socket,
Flashed once and screamed, the delightful Miss Muppet,
If she had waited to pass on to heaven,
Today was her birthday, she would have been seven!

3 March 2008

Would He Even Know Me Now?

The past is full of shades and shapes
Of people, come and gone,
'Whatever happened to so and so,'
We say, when the mood is on;
But closer still, our parents live
In the warmth of our hearts and minds,
And my father often returns to me
To haunt my quiet times.

How do you deal with a love so deep
That it tears your life apart?
The day that he left, he took a piece
Of my ever caring heart,
He died, and so did I that day,
But I couldn't even cry,
A loss so great to a fickle fate -
I wept, though my eyes were dry.

Though that was twenty years ago
I remember in every way,
He'll always be just the way he was
On that final, desperate day;
But I have changed, I'm older now
And life has never been kind,
The years have indelibly traced their path
On my face, my body and mind.

My father knew me way back when,
A child, a teen, young man,

I hovered around the forty mark
When he left in the Lord's great plan;
But one thing worries my troubled mind
And it haunts my thoughts somehow,
If we were to pass on the street today
Would he even know me now?

5 March 2008

Getting Old

Now that we're suddenly old and tired,
The mirrors are never as kind,
We venture out in a world that changed
As our youth slipped far behind;
We only walk at a snail's pace
And shiver in autumn rain,
Then stop to rest, as the evening light
Draws down on us, once again.

The young look on, but they never see
They'll be old one day, like us,
They think we live in some cobweb dream
And just fade away, and rust;
When I come in from the world outside
And shutter the outer door,
I see my lover still waits for me
As she's done so often before.

I tend to gaze at her longer now,
To capture her in my mind,

We're not too sure of the time we've got
So we tend to be more than kind,
I kiss her gently and watch the glow
Of stars, at the back of her eyes,
And she opens up like a flower in spring
At a touch, or a sweet surprise.

Then many an evening, after dark
When the wind howls up at the moon,
I gently unwrap my sweetest gift
And rest my face in the gloom,
She sighs and soughs like a gentle breeze,
Leans back like a sapling bent,
And touch is a pit at the end of the world
Where our last few days are spent.

5 March 2008

While I Write and Breathe…

Every time
I hold this pen
I feel some moving spirit stir,
Like mist in distant valleys, pouring
Down from Snowdon's druid lair.

Down along
The deep Welsh valleys,
Through the blood of ancient cells,
Seeking, ever seeking knowledge,
Stored within the Book of Kells.

Late at night
I well remember
You, hunched at your crystal ball,
Gazing ever deep at shadows,
Haunting you, from times before.

Born from out
The Mabinogi,
Steeped in myth and songs unsung,
Caught your whispered Celtic tales from
Taliesin's silvered tongue.

Once you rose
In Aberavon,
Building fires before the dawn,
You, long weaned on dragon's milk
Could spell each witch, or evil-born.

When you grew
They travelled with you,
Dreams and myths and second sight,
Gypsies turned and crossed themselves
When meeting you at past-midnight.

You, who taught me
How to scribe
The signs and portents of our fate,
I hold the pen, you hold my hand
And pen the words I dissipate.

Though you've gone
To roam the valleys,
Haunt the chalets of your kin,

I see you stare from out the crystal,
Every time my gaze stares in.

Mother, you are
Old and weathered,
Long gone from this mortal shore,
Still your blood revives my palate,
Paints your colours at my core.

Paints your colours,
Chants your passions
Traces all your patterns here,
You will never be forgotten
While I write and breathe, my dear!

8 March 2008

I Must Have Been Sleeping

'Where are you going,' I heard her say
As the dream took me straight to the core,
We parked at the side of a very long road
And I got out the driver's door;
'I've never known that,' I replied, and she sat
On her hands, with the pain of surprise,
'So what you've been saying has never been true!'
The tears rose up in her eyes!

'The road has been long, the road has been wide,
I never knew where I could turn.'
'I thought you were happy with me,' she said;
There was nothing to say in return.

'I must have been sleeping for seventeen years,'
My voice sounded foreign and coarse,
But I couldn't handle the sighs and the lies,
Or the terrible sound of - 'divorce!'

I walked to the wood at the side of the road,
And followed the pathway around,
I couldn't look back now I'd made up my mind
Though I walked unfamiliar ground,
The clearing was quiet, the birds didn't sing,
A mountain rose up in my view,
I suddenly saw there was no going back
To the comfortable life that I knew.

I cast off my shackles and took a deep breath,
To breathe in both freedom and pride,
My strength was returning, and clearer my eye,
I walked with a bounce in my stride,
The years fell away, I was thirty again,
I stopped then, and sat on a stone,
For darkness was gathering there in the gloom
With that terrible feeling - alone!

I thought of the woman I'd left on the road,
Who'd always been faithful to me,
The tears that she'd shed for a love that was dead
Made me sad, and ashamed to be free,
I thought of the comfort she'd given me when
All my world started going insane,
She'd cooked and she'd cared,
                    and she'd loved and she'd shared
And I'd given her nothing but pain.

I turned on the track, and I made my way back
But I couldn't see where I had been,
I stumbled through thickets and walked into trees
And I fell on my knees on the green.
'I am lost, I am lost,' I cried into the night
Then I heard her voice, dim, by a tree,
And woke to her stroking my face and my brow
As I cried… She was waiting for me!

9 March 2008

Winter Comes…

Where once the spring
Shone in our faces,
Tugged at our heart-strings
Danced at our traces,
Now there are chills,
Portents inside us,
Shadows from far-off hills
Now walk beside us.

Love came and went,
Followed its calling,
Left us to rue the chance-glance
Of each falling,
Tears followed laughter,
Sadness brought pain,
Love flowed down gutters
With every spring rain.

What of the children
Laughing beside us?
Spring turned to summer
And quickly denied us;
Scorched our intentions
And scratched all our itches;
Where are the children now?
Hedgerows and ditches!

So much for summer, one
Long dissipation,
Autumn leaves spiral
And pile desolation,
Deep in our hearts those old
Tears are still falling,
Dark clouds are gathering
As winter comes calling.

15 March 2008

Woman

Woman, Oh Woman,
Why do you try me,
Why do you shake me,
Break me
Deny me
When all that you do
Is deride and defy me?

Once we were young
And you painted your faces,

Pierced your tongues
And silk-stockinged your traces;
Wafted the scent of despair
And seduction,
Coloured your lips with
A hint of corruption,
Taunted and teased with your hips
As they swayed it,
Aimed at my reason;
Dismayed and waylaid it.

I was bemused
By your willful distraction,
Caught in your spell
And the well of attraction,
Courted and charmed
As you played 'hard to get me',
Turned my face from you
As much as you'd let me,
Filled you with praises
Then watched you cuckold me,
Took to another
So she could just hold me.

Year followed year
And your scent, it still lingers,
Once I stood tall and strong,
Now I'm all fingers,
Love came and went until
I was but sated,
Everything failed
Then you came to me, naked,
Now in the twilight

We look on and wonder
Where are the ties that bind?
All torn asunder!

Woman, oh Woman,
Why do you sigh me,
Why do you shake me
Break me
And cry me,
When all that you want is
To lie here beside me?

30 March 2008

Skipping!

A little girl was skipping;
As she swung her skipping rope
The neighbors heard her singing
And the song she sang was - Quote:

'Mummy's in the parlour
And she's there with Uncle Fred,
Daddy's in the garage
Says she's doing in his head,
Auntie Jane was crying
Now she's swimming in the pool
And I must keep on skipping
'Til it's time to go to school.'

The neighbors saw her skipping
All along the afternoon,
She skipped a hundred singles
As she sang her little tune:

'Mummy's saying nothing
But she hasn't any clothes,
Uncle Fred is staring
With a chopper through his nose,
Auntie Jane is floating
But her face is turning black
And Daddy's in the garage
With a rope around his neck.'

A little girl was skipping
But there wasn't any sound,
I guess she'll still be skipping
When the sun goes down…

1 April 2008.

What's in a Name?

My friend, Olly Dee, is a funny old card,
He could have been so many things,
A builder, an architect, surgeon, a cop,
A soldier, a pilot with wings;
In fact, he did nothing at all with his life,
Not one little thing did he do,
He spent all his time meditating at large,
And blaming his mother, at Loo.

Someone once said: - 'What's in a name?'
It's simply a patent disguise -
But Oll has a brother, who's simply a Fred,
Who's just won the Nobel Prize.

One time, long ago, Olly filled out a form
To prove that he really was there,
A letter came, postmarked the palace at dawn
To say that they'd made him a 'Sir'.

He never could face writing in for a job,
Or sitting his licence to drive,
His tax is a mess, and he's changed his address
Seven times before agents arrive.
There's never enough of a space on the page
When it's - 'Sign - or risk paying a fee,'
For Oliver Cavendish Norton FitzWalter
John Lindisfarne Ackerman Dee.

8 May 2008

WWW.

At night, I sit in this darkened room
And stare at the hollow screen,
The World-Wide Web is a crystal ball
Of tides, and hopes, and dreams,
Though the world goes on outside my door
And time, it flows like the sea,
I have no truck with reality
When the web washes over me.

For I dredge the depths with a grappling hook
And I haul my catch on board,
Then I read the thoughts of a million minds
That were left on the furthest shore,

While the colours swirl and the lights go dim
And the sounds fade from without,
I float in the mass of cyberspace
'Til the light of the moon goes out.

Then emails beat at my cyber door
To ask if I'll let them in,
I cast my net for the viruses,
And choke the Recycle bin,
I stare at faces I've never seen
That float on a cyber wave,
Which disappear as the next comes near
For the two are never the same.

But one returns, and it stares at me
And I see the limpid eyes,
Like pools in deep lagoons offshore
Where the mermaid lives and dies,
While the lips are full of promises
As false as the deepest sin,
I reach on out to the screen, but find
That the screen won't let me in.

Then night on night, like a dread parade
Those pictures come again,
From some lost ancient URL
Long gone from the world of men,
I search and Google in cyberspace
In hopes that you're somewhere there,
But all I have are those limpid eyes
And the bands in your dark brown hair.

One night, I'll leap right through the screen
And swim to your blue lagoon,
I'll take bright garlands of pretty flowers

To gladden the cyber gloom,
We'll live forever behind the screen
And our faces will go online,
For the stares of the grim night dwellers
Who are surfing the Web, World-Wide.

10 June 2008

Isabel Allende

I did but see you once, and that
Upon some distant screen,
You spoke of life and love, and death,
And wickedness, supreme;
Your eyes reflected truth and pain,
Of life's relentless round,
Where happiness is one brief glimpse
Before death puts us down.

You spoke of your dear daughter
How she passed within your arms,
How sudden stillness stayed your grief
And soothed your vague alarms,
You fear not death, nor even life
You said, and won my heart,
For such as you inspire the few
Too timid to depart.

Your face reflects the aura
That we see in ancient saints,
Like Joan of Arc, you fight each cause,
Ignore mankind's restraints,

The lessons of your life have left
A glow within your mind,
Of fire and ice, behind the eyes
Of troubled womankind.

1 July 2008

What Happened to the Day?

'My child, what is that sound I hear,
That rush of many feet?
I hear the people gathering
Tumultuous in the street,
I hear the people shouting
But I can't hear what they say,
The sun begins to set, my child,
What happened to the day?'

'I well remember waking, it
Was such a glorious dawn,
The clouds splashed red and tumbling
From Dante's palette born;
The clouds so red, it hurt my eyes
I had to look away,
Why look you so forlorn, my child,
What happened to the day?'

My memory has failed once more,
Again, it's taken wing,
You must remind these weary bones,
I don't recall a thing.
The clouds reflected through the house
Some sense of red dismay,

I ask you once again, my child,
What happened to the day?'

'My wife, my love of fifty years
Came out and smiled at me,
I sat her in her favourite chair
And then I let her be.
She doesn't always know me now,
Her mind has gone away,
Who are these men in uniform...
What happened to the day?'

'You keep reflecting on the blade
That's lying on my lap,
I must have carved the luncheon roast -
I can't remember that!
There's blood all over everywhere
But how, I couldn't say,
My child, my mind's beyond repair,
What happened to the day?

'I only acted out of love,
Whatever else is true,
If I could just remember
What it was I had to do?
These men are treating me so rough,
They're taking me away,
Your eyes are hard and cold, my child,
What happened to the day?'

17 October 2008

The Attic

'There's nobody in
But the light is on
And a chair just creaked,
Did you hear it, son?
There's been no chairs
For ever so long,
So who's abroad
In the attic, son?'

'That grim old lady
Who haunts the stairs
In a faded dress
With a world of cares,
Whenever I look
She disappears,
But lives in a world
That's drowned in tears.'

'They say she mutters
Beneath the moon
From the window there
In the month of June,
The light was out
In that ancient room
When she jumped from the window,
Into the gloom.'

'Why does she haunt
The attic, son,
If her soul took flight
When the moon was gone?
What is she trying
To tell us, son?'

'There's nobody in
But the light is on!'

26 October 2008

The Melbourne Cup

That's it, I quit! I'm through, straight up!
Once more, I flunked the Melbourne Cup!
I'll go and sit where dunces sit,
And swear this time that - That is it!

That bloody horse that weaved on through
To snatch the cup, some name like 'View',
I never even saw it there
It wasn't on the list, I swear!

I think they subbed it in at dawn
So punters wouldn't know its form,
Then hid it 'til the race was run
Confusing almost everyone.

Now every year it's been the same
Since 'Think Big' blew them all away,
They suck us in to have a punt
Then pull them, and let through a runt.

It's one great big conspiracy
To part me from my shekel tree,
But that's the end, and that I swear...
(I wonder who will win next year?)

5 November 2008

Titan

Parodies and caricatures are the most
penetrating of criticisms

- Aldous Huxley -

'Point Counter Point'

You, with all your art
And neat device,
Your sense of self
And engineering skills,
Determined					5
With emotion set aside,
You'd leave your Titan sprawled
On our poetic hills.

Your Titan, sprawled
And rusted now with age,				10
That bleeds its rust each year
Upon the land,
To waste the lilacs, starved
Of sun and light,
And breed new crops,				15
Your waste, your contraband.

False prophet you, who fooled
A people once,
Who, godlike, thought to stifle
Us at heart,					20
Used as your tool cold reason
So precise,
And sordid captions
On some other's art.

 You taught us how to steal			25
- not plagiarize;
You taught us how to steal

Not imitate,
Damn your eyes!

Tiresias now walks alone in Birmingham   30
Takes bitter by the pint, as is his wont,
Adjusts his wrinkled tie when he is charming 'em
And tells 'em of the tide at Hellespont,
(The tide he's never seen), at Hellespont.

  What roots are there in this,   35
  What branches grow
  Out of this stony rubbish?

The Titan glares and rusts in the sun,
The Titan glares –
Each rusted nut and bolt I'd see undone;   40
Each rusted bolt.

(The Titan glares!)

Jen ne veux pas vous parler dans votre langue,
Pourquoi voulez-vous me parler dans la mienne?

You may not seek to turn again   45
You may not seek,
You may not turn, but find undone
The vanished power of the unusual brain;
The rat's foot
On the funereal urn.   50

At the violet hour, they took us to the bridge
And showed us proudly round the gleaming brass,
Then cracked a coldy each, from out the fridge

While Phlebas patted Mrs. Porter's ass.

And every horficer wore belt and braid 55
And swaggered, or just stood there, looking proud
'Til someone shivered, lookin' at the mist
And Belladonna laughed, a little loud.

'This way now, gents – and Mrs. P.,
The mangelwurzel soup will cool 60
If we should but delay, you see
Now; single file and follow me,'

All this I knew, when I was young
All this I knew;

Ipso facto 65
Mumbo jumbo
Too wit,
Tereu.

The floor she sat on, like a burning bone
Gleamed in the sheen of Fisher's Wax, 70
The cleaning lady had long gone home
To sort out her husband's income-tax.
So there she sat in her plastic pearls
To drink from a vial of coloured glass,
Of coloured glass. 75

The Titan stirs, and glares with rheumy eyes
And tries to see the narrow path we trod,
Then shakes his head, unwilling to believe
That Dead is God.

O
What shall we do
The wind is rushing through
And I am blown
      hither;
I am blown
      thither;

    War is ein Geister?

Oh, if we but knew
What we do
When we delve or hew;
Within this sacred wood
What desecration
Did you do?

Walk in
Between the Titan and the land,
Observe the barren aspect of its line,
Perceive, along the shadow of its hand
This verse of mine.

Like some lit city
Majestic, floating
Surrounded by night,
The sound of revels
All care uncaring
You led this loud
  Deceiving flight.

You led them, unfeeling
As drunks through wet gutters,

You squandered them, stealing
From all as you went,
You taught them to turn down 110
The lights, close the shutters
And took from them more than
The vision you lent.

Son of man
You only know 115
A heap of broken images,
Where the sun beats
And praise dies
Turning to grimaces.

Jug jug, 120

There I saw one I knew
And I stopped him there, crying
'You! – Jackson – who was with me
In the ditch at My Lai,
How many were shot 125
Did you count all the dying,
But he turned from me quickly
To re-frame his reply.

(Because he knows that time is always time,
For one time, and one place, 130
A place is not a place before that time;
Which time is yet to come – I see
Confusion in his face).

HURRY UP PLEASE, IT'S TIME

Think. Think. Do you never think?　　　　　　135
If you think, speak, speak to me – speak!

We're none of us the same, the boys reply;
Do you not feel, are you not moved within?
Does nothing bring about the flush of change?

Emotion is pernicious! Don't cloud your mind　　140
With feel. Think!
Perceive –
Sensibility, sensitivity,
Don't feel!
Blink Blink.　　　　　　　　　　　　　　　145
(The ways of God are strange!)

My old man said follow the van
And don't dilly dally on the way,
Off went the van with me 'ome packed in it,
I walked be'ind with me old cock linnet –　　150

And when the Archduke, my mentor
Took me out to ski in a bed,
He said:
'Whee, hang on tight Marie – and down he went.
I breed, much of the night,　　　　　　　　155
And go south in the winter.

Wir tanzten im Wintergarten im Regen –
Durch den Berlinen Nachten, mein Liebchen,
Durch den Berlinen Nachten.
Kannst du dich daran errinern…?　　　　　　160

　- and all the conversations sound the same.

Under the brown moon of a winter smog
Mr. Homogenes, the urgent surgeon,
Adjusted his spectacles
And sat on the bog. 165

At the violet hour
Of the purple passages
The typist returns
With a pack full of packages,
De-frosts the fricassee 170
And separates the sausages,
But longs to be ravished
By a small bunch of radishes.

I've heard it all before, I've heard
The long, the short, the tall of it, 175
I've heard the ho hum,
And the fee fi fo fum of it,
In the mornings
And through the long-drawn afternoons –
I shall wear my trousers rolled in macaroons. 180

And so it goes on
And on
And on, and on;
And so it beams its wisdom
Down the years, 185
The inimitable dichotomy
Of the uttermost monotony.

Gratias tibi maximus Catullas
Agit pessimus omnium poeta.

    I think!   190
    Blink Blink.

Call it not vain; they do not err
Who say, that when the poet dies
Mute nature mourns her worshipper –
(She may be mute – but nature lies!)   195

'A quick one round the ballroom with you dear,'
(He'd grovel if he thought that it would please),
'Oh, ain't it fun, I'm glad I came this year…'
'Step quickly now – (and let me glimpse yer knees).'

'It's like a palace, ain't it – you're from Leeds?'   200
(I never liked that 'ole) – 'Well I'm from Brum.
Yes, I'm in brushes – 'lectric ones and leads,
A working trip I'm on -' (Let's feel yer bum).

'It's so sophisticated, ain't it now?
Would you be in a cabin on yer own?   205
Oh, dearie me, that's 'andy' – that ole cow!
Still, even Mrs. P's been seen to roam.

She smoothes her skirt with automatic hand
And fixes her hair with a tortoiseshell comb
Then leads him to her cabin, on demand –   210
And lets him have his way
While she fiddles with the telephone.

    Row row row the boat
    Gently out to sea
    Merrily merrily merrily merrily….   215

The First Class are letting go tonight, Captain,
The First Class are kicking up their heels;
They won't forget tonight, I'll lay you odds
                    Mein Kapitan
They won't forget tonight.   220

They'll mark this night
Along the lonely years,
When they were cool
And didn't stop to blink,
When all was intellect and reason;   225
Drink your beers,
Drink up, I feel the cold

- Don't feel, just think!

When woman stoops to take her brolly
In the rain,   230
And wanders down
The Kaiser Wilhelmstrasse,
She's careful not to glance
The way she came,
Fur den angezogenen Korper in dem grasse.   235

She paints her face, and saunters
Like a whore
Which lights der kerzen Leuchter
At Frau Meiers,
Whose very moral eyes will seek   240
Beyond her door;
The young flesh
For her aging fires.

(What this has begun
They'll all carry on,   245
For sixty odd years
They'll all carry on
Carry on).

Jug jug.

She lay awake   250
And stared at stars
Not feeling now;
He snored beside her –
Stuck for conversation;
She stared at stars   255
She stared at stars
And didn't think
She lay awake.

The Titan rolled, and turned to look behind.
What comes behind, what   260
Comes behind
What comes?

   What went before
   Now comes behind –
   A new dawn breaks.   265

Jug Jug
Woo Woo
Tereu.

The mist was down so long, I didn't see it.

The mist it was – we couldn't see
Don't look at me!

A dry brain
In a dry season
Beating oars
Elizabeth and Leicester,
A rat's feet
On dry bones
That lay too long
By Cirencester.

How many boats have we got, Captain
How many boats?
How many miles to home, chaplain –
    Mein Herr Kapitan?

Between the meter and the scan
Between the poet and the man
Lies the shadow.

Between the iceberg and the keel
Between the intellect and feel
The depth is shallow.

Between the dawn and then the night
Between the left thigh and the right –
Marshmallow!

A woman drew her long black hair out white,
And screamed – 'We never knew that we were had;
We never knew…'

Don't think, you might just feel
Don't think, don't feel
Lock anguish at your breast –

'Too late, for you will all go down with me,'
She moaned, 300
Caught in some feeling reverie –
Too late
Too late
You'll all go down with me.

   Te Deum. 305

The boats have gone
The boats have gone
They will desert us
Every one.

Shall I set my lands in ruins 310
All these fragments

   They have bored me to my bruins!

(Die fasten glanzen
Und rost ein bischen mehr).

Ile fight you for it! 315

   Bosch! Why would you care?

Ditto Ditto Ditto

Tereu

Te Deum.

29-30 September 1982

(with no apologies to T.S. Eliot)

Notes on Titan

The title of this work was chosen for the reason that it very aptly parodies T.S. Eliot's 'The Waste Land' and other poems, both in the vastness of its bulk, and on its effect on the poetry of the last ninety years. It is also no accident that the narrative parallels the voyage of the 'Titanic'.

'Titan' is a parody, and should be read as such. I make no claims for it to be either a great, or original, work of art.

The following notes are provided to give credit where it is due, and to point the finger where it is not.

In the theft of the many and various lines I follow the master's advice, taken from his essay on Masinger - the text is at note #4 below.

I owe nothing to Miss Weston's book on the Grail Legend. Indeed, I have never read it. The same may be said of 'The Golden Bough', and the only vegetation ceremonies I know of were those used in the construction of Eliot's original poems.

If my notes seem copious, they do at least explain in part. Eliot's notes tended to mystify. For this reason, I must necessarily, like Eliot, though in a different manner, treat you all as idiots!

David Lewis Paget

1. line 6 - 'The end of the enjoyment of poetry is a pure contemplation from which all the accidents of personal emotion are removed.' T.S. Eliot - 'The Perfect Critic.'

2. l.13 - 'April is the cruelest month, breeding
    Lilacs out of the dead land.' WL-l.-1/2

3. l. 19-22 - 'We assume the gift of a superior sensibility.' - 'The Perfect Critic.'

4. l. 25-28 - 'One of the surest of tests is the way in which a poet borrows. Immature poets imitate; mature poets steal.' - Essay on Masinger.

5. l. 30 - Teresias, Eliot's central character, transported here to Birmingham to live out a sordid old age.

6. l. 33 - The Hellespont, now called the Dardanelles. The scene of the legend of Hero and Leander - also the scene of the legendary swim of Lord Byron.

7. l. 35 - In WL this reads:
    'What are the roots that clutch.'

8. l. 43-44 - 'I do not wish to converse in your language,
    Why should you wish to converse in mine?'

9. l. 45 - From - 'Because I do not hope to turn again.' (Ash Wednesday)

10. l. 54 - Phlebas, Eliot's drowned Phoenician, here seen before the event with Mrs. Porter; that same Mrs. Porter who, with her daughter, 'wash their feet in soda water.'

11. l. 58 - Belladonna - Eliot's adapted Tarot Card, 'The Lady of the Rocks.' Appropriate in this situation, in the mist.

12. l. 65-68 - Ipso-facto - by virtue of the same fact, or, Ipse Dixit, Humpty Dumpty - substitute to taste.

13. l. 69 - Here Eliot's 'Anthony and Cleopatra' theft is further transformed in some surrealistic lunacy.

14. l. 79 - Also interchangeable, but in its present form relates more firmly to Eliot perceived.

15. l. 80-86 - The winds of change in poetry, which 'The Waste Land' set in motion.

16. l. 87 - Was it a ghost?

17. l. 88-90 - From 'Binsey Poplars' by Gerard Maney Hopkins.

18. l. 91 - 'The Sacred Wood', Eliot's dissertation on modern criticism.

19. l. 114-117 - Son of man
>You cannot say, or guess, for you know only
>A heap of broken images, where the sun beats'
>(Lines 20-22 WL).

20. l. 122 - "You who were with me in the ships at Mylae.' (l. 70 WL)

21. l. 125 - From verse 3 of 'Ash Wednesday'.

22. l. 130 - The barman from 'A Game of Chess.' WL

23. l. 131 - 'Speak to me. Why do you never speak? Speak?
(Line 112 - WL)

24. l. 133 - From 'They' - Siegfried Sassoon.

25. l. 136-140 - 'It is one more instance of the pernicious effect of emotion.' - 'The Perfect Critic.'

26. l. 142 - Also from 'They' - Siegfried Sassoon.

27. l. 143 - Old Music Hall song.

28. l. 147-151 -
'And when we were children, staying at the Archduke's
My cousins, he took me out on a sled
And I was frightened. He said Marie,
Marie, Hold on tight. And down we went.
In the mountains there, you feel free.
I read, much of the night, and go south in the winter.' - WL

29. l. 152-155 - 'We danced the Wintergarden in the rain
Oh those Berlin nights, my sweet
Those Berlin nights.
Do you remember...'

30. l. 157-160 - 'Under the brown fog of a winter noon
Mr Eugenides, the Smyrna merchant
Unshaven, with a pocket full of currants' - etc.
Lines 208-210 WL

31. l. 161 - 'At the violet hour, the evening hour that strives
Homeward, and brings the sailor home from sea,
The typist home at teatime, clears her breakfast, lights
Her stove and lays food out in tins.'
$$\text{Lines 220-223 WL}$$

32. l. 167-168 - 'Well now that's done, and I'm glad it's over.'
$$\text{Line 252 WL}$$

33. l. 169-172 - 'For I have known them all already, known them all -
Have known the evenings, mornings, afternoons.'
$$\text{'The Love Song of Alfred J. Prufrock.'}$$

34. l. 173 - 'I grow old... I grow old...
I shall wear the bottoms of my trousers rolled.' Cf.

35. l. 181-182 - 'Catallus, the worst of all poets
Gives you his warmest thanks.' (Carmina xlix)
(Here, you too, the reader, may be erudite with a
copy of the Penguin Dictionary of Quotations).

36. l. 185-187 - 'The Lay of the Last Minstrel' (Vi) Sir Walter Scott.

37. l. 188 - The fourth line is mine. His reads:
'And celebrates his obsequies.'

38. l. 201 - 'She smooths her hair with automatic hand
And puts a record on the gramophone.'
$$\text{l. 255-6 WL.}$$

39. l. 206-208 - Old song: line 2 should read 'Gently up the stream' - but in this sense 'out to sea' is more apt.

40. l. 209 - Those, in 1922, who went all out in favour of the form'lessness) of 'The Waste Land'. The beginning of the 'exclusive audience' for poetry.

41. l. 221 - '...as sensibility is rare, unpopular and desirable, it is to be expected that the critic and the creative artist should frequently be the same person.' - 'The Perfect Critic.'

42. l. 222 - 'When lovely woman stoops to folly and
              Paces about her room again, alone.'
This was taken in turn from:
         'When lovely woman stoops to folly
         And finds too late that men betray,
         What charms can soothe her melancholy,
         What art can wash her guilt away?'
(The Vicar of Wakefield - Oliver Goldsmith).

43. l. 243-251 - 'The time is now propitious, as he guesses,
           The meal is ended, she is bored and tired,
           Endeavours to engage her in caresses
           Which still are unreproved, if undesired.'
                                      l. 235-238 WL

44. l. 262-264 - Any reference to the 'Titanic' through various passages may be taken as read.

45. l. 265-266 - From 'Gerontion.' - T.S.E.

46. l. 267-268 - Lines 279-280 inverted. WL.

47. l. 269-270 - 'And bones cast in a little low, dry garret
            Rattled by the rat's foot only, year to year.
                                  Lines 194-195 WL

48. l. 277-285 - 'Between the conception
    And the creation
    Between the emotion
    And the response,
    Falls the shadow' etc.
       (The Hollow Men - T.S.E.)

49. l. 286 - 'A woman drew her long black hair out tight.' (l. 377 - WL)

50. l. 289 - 'Eliot's style is carefully impersonal.'
    (David Craig - 'The Defeatism of the Waste Land.')

51. l. 303 - 'Shall I at least set my lands in order?' (l. 425 - WL)

52. l. 304 - 'These fragments I have shored against my ruins.'
       (l. 430 - WL)

53. l. 308-309 - 'Why then Ile fit you. Hieronymo's mad againe.'
       (l. 431 - WL)

54. l. 310 - His end is 'Shantih Shantih Shantih' - explained as 'the peace which 'passeth understanding' - (pretty much like his poem!)

Footnote - Perhaps I shall be criticised for taking Eliot's critical utterings, and ascribing them to Eliot the poet. To excuse myself in part, I repeat Eliot's statement at the end of 'The Perfect Critic.'

'...it is to be expected that the critic and the creative artist should frequently be the same person.'

       David Lewis Paget

Index of First Lines

Abis, Ackerman, Benson and Blunt	86
A crane stands gaunt against the sky	44
A few short lines informed us you were dead	239
A girl, not young	301
Ah!... Ah!... What is man	129
A light appeared on the darkest hill	207
A little girl was skipping	409
'All curses on this pen	250
All I can offer you	110
All my futures	185
All my life was laid to waste, the	72
All things burn slowly	254
All you left were your plastic pieces	284
And did those feet	327
And so, and so	304
And so to this, then	147
And so to you my sweet, it comes	342
And what strange time is this	299
And when you were a lover	93
And when you were a seesaw	94
And when you were a young girl	92
And you, my father	291
Another year ended	289
Anything's possible, Sweetness and Light	111
A raindrop from the womb am I	19
Armourless fool to emotion I am	53
A scanner in Greenland relaying the score	27
As I recall, when we were young	83
As I was driving slowly by	148
As night it comes down, feather deep	319
At life's butt end, I offer this, my sweet	323

At night, I sit in this darkened room	411
At one with me, this silence	300
At what lame moment	271
At Granite Island's seaward side	231
Before the British Fleet sailed out	252
Before the mountains	81
Both Zhang and Tao, and Wang and Chen	353
Bron Dilys Teashop	234
By fields and by coppice	262
Cast no dark shadows	111
'Come on Jim, we'll earn a bob	60
Corporal Corporal	58
Darling girl, will you love me now	115
Dim figures from the mists walk at my wall	256
'Don't grumble and growl and roar at me	132
Do you ever get that feeling, that	174
'Do you think that I'm Captain Marvel	176
Driving in starlight	102
Each night	203
Each time you left	311
Each winter the grey-greying streets of Pengellen	279
English is simple, it flitters from the tongue	369
Every time	402
Find me a coast where the sea rolls in	25
Five children I	244
For part of your voyage, Captain	333
For some is death	141
From a blue cloud at the two o'clock	272
From Monday through to Friday, and	367
From trench to trench	320
'Get rid of those old shoes,' she said	397
'Goal!' he yelled, and laughed up at the sun	210
Good God Almighty	386

Green is the wych-elm	192
Grey old lady, sat by the sea	124
Have ever you looked and seen the smile	101
Have ever you seen	178
Here I am, sixty one	349
Here I am, twenty-one	142
Her hair was as black as a starling's tail	362
He's laid his head on a Chinese street	384
He slept through the Paleozoic age	389
He's steeped in the shadows of ivy and stone	134
High cliffs and rock pools	263
His eyes are sharp, and glitter	52
How many men march, tramp	88
How much further to Warwick?	21
'How much we change	287
How sleepless the night	161
I break my back on many a rock	31
I cannot stay, I cannot go	378
I can see the pit of darkness stretched	127
I did but see you once, and that	413
'I died early,' said the Spirit	23
'I don't love you anymore	205
I dripped my blood on the final word	70
I drove you through the mistlands	103
If all I gave	223
If all my words	216
If all the world were pen and ink	88
If he once knew the light, it has not been	259
If 'I CAN' can, it's done right away	370
If I had loved them all, as I love you	325
If I had time to think	314
I find it strange that one as versed as you	255
If, in the end	149

If I should disappear one sudden night	348
If life was only	251
If you die, I shall smash all the windows	145
I had a fright the other night	372
I have a dog called Harry	395
I have left my heart	378
I have no words, nor patterns left	316
I have sought our scattered scenes	285
I hope, one day, you'll read this, son	59
I knelt to peer at my brother's face	67
I lay a-dream in Byron Bay	84
I'm only the flotsam, jetsam drift	131
I'm shivering in the afterglow	48
I'm trapped within my past of English days	149
I'm waiting for a number nine	51
I, my friend	268
In April 1770, 'Endeavour' put to sea	45
In Chantris Lane I caught a glimpse	80
In every word, in every smile	225
In the days of our beginnings when this	112
In the half twilight of my empty year	385
In the year of the Jade Emperor	356
I pen this creed for those we leave behind	208
I rose at this a.m. and caught the phone	341
I sang in the choir when I was young	387
I saw the cloud in the morning sky	74
I see black moods of cloudy thought	117
I seem to recollect a certain	139
I see with eyes	165
I sit and stare at this empty page	345
Islands of memories	130
I spun the car in a squealing turn	159
I staggered out of the Monkey Ba	379

I stand alone on Wentworth Hill	18
I stand alone that you are not alone	241
I stand marooned at life's most distant shore	218
Is this your home acre	217
I take my seat at the Golden Grove	354
I thought to write of love	206
'I thought you would learn by this	136
It is not ours to seek to trace	162
It's all I can do to remember	173
It's a weary life, my lady	199
It's better for some than for others	125
It's cold and damp in the light of day	97
It won't do you any good	82
It would not snow at Wessex Bridge	17
I've been for a stroll by the midnight beach	129
'I've failed!' How many times have sons	151
I've founded a club for our frustrated poets	55
I've heard all the scratched plastic carols	126
I've heard your most familiar voice	150
'I've noticed that light before,' she said	53
I've no use	171
I've often thought that all the time	152
I've run out of tales for the telling	109
I've said before that I'd like to go	76
I've sat and I've wondered for night after night	118
I've seen it in the mirrors that	211
I've seen three starlings in the sun-set	110
I've walked at your ruins	265
I've watched your children, playing in the sand	366
I walked to the back verandah	339
'I would like, good sirs	41
Jeannie, what have you done to me	106
Jennifer Absalom Maudlin-Mand	399

Jiao Ba Lu is an ancient street	375
John Bryce set sail on a winter's morn	38
Last night I heard a Chinese song	394
Life, a Play	278
Long since I sailed me	258
Love is some trick	308
May you ply your trade in the morning	100
Merlin-magic, mixing potions	43
Milady Gay whose	222
Must I forever take the past	243
My brain has turned to ash, and yes	308
'My child, what is that sound I hear	414
My friend, Olly Dee, is a funny old card	410
My lady, you once sought my drift	230
My memory's shell-shocked standard flies	164
My mind is musty, overgrown	80
My mother's folk were miners	63
My wife has walked away with herself again	42
Nights in white cottages	243
No longer knowing what or who I am	294
No longer young, I trace my spin	247
Now that we're suddenly old and tired	401
Of all the lines	226
'Oh, it's not that I want to be awkward	119
'Oh, woman in child	158
Once more I mark	302
On distant tors, in ancient Keeps	186
One heart's ache ended	273
Out of the nightmare came a dream	78
Rad Morgan came riding beside our fair city	189
Remember this, my son	296
Romany girl on the silver sand	103
Sat at the edge of a rickety boat that is	105

Scene from a Yamaha	87
Set me out forewarned	335
She moves within	212
She ventured out from her castle walls	96
Sir John de Vere has took a quill	194
Soft scattered at	216
Some cryptic line has told your time	191
Some ride high pacers	293
So these old grey bones are dead, Saturn	90
So this is your warren of secrets	321
So you told your closest friends that you're	116
Stark patterns rent by winter storms	198
Stars clash, and pale moons	229
Steel grey above	303
Still and grey in death he lies	20
'Surprize........Surprize'	37
That's it, I quit! I'm through, straight up	418
The basic tenets of my faith	253
'The best you left with me	298
The black-haired girls are graceful, like gazelles	352
The cat and I stare at the room	347
The China stint is over	382
'The colour has run from your shirt,' I said	155
'The creaking hulks of rotten, rat-infested vermin	34
The earth's beginning to creak and groan	393
The first dawn breaks	140
The great themes are ended	286
The heart is still, there is no pounding at this beach	324
The mad churl at the headstone	183
The old King lay in the shadow	158
The past is full of shades and shapes	400
The past is neatly shed	221
The poet lives up on a windy hill	26

There are no answers to your questionings	329
There is no fate that	188
There is no love like the sea brings	292
There is the family photograph	179
There once was time to sit and spin	306
There's a distant drift of tides	330
There's an old coast, an old coast	266
There's nobody in	416
There's something a-move in your mind, girl	104
There was a bright-eyed boy	340
The sand remains, but naught, my love, of you	223
The sea of storms came in	312
The sea shore is the gods lap	190
The season is heralded first by the trees	30
These cheque book eyes that peer on out	343
These winter days have been long and cold	157
The skies are empty and grey at dawn	350
The sun dipped into a puddle	181
The tide has dumped me in some trough	202
The time shortens	201
The worlds I sought and thought to win	228
They squeak, and rattle, and jerk, and pull	360
This dream has ravelled at the edge	165
This is the year the gods will play in	344
This land of ancients grows on me	350
This poet grows grey bearded	276
This thirty-seventh year is made complete	245
This world unravels, bit by bit	232
Too often in this gaping land	154
We come from Shoreditch	33
We have grown old	236
We overplayed and underplayed our parts	309
We seem condemned to partings, you and I	325

We stare at the rocks and shoreline	332
We stared the night at stars, as in a dream	233
We touch things we see not	98
We, who may but sit and fret	254
What	231
What day is ours	269
What did you mean	297
What ever happens when a love goes wrong	146
What futile webs our journeys weave	187
'What have you done to your head again?'	133
What have you left me	219
What long dread phantom	237
What miners art	264
What now is my faded country	307
What's in a name, 'Lady Shore'	36
What sort of wild temptress is this	202
What spark in you	281
What thought fear burns	180
What will you do now, Peter Brown	115
What would you with me	282
What ya gonna do	168
When all the threads are broken	215
Whenever I dreamed, I seemed to set	184
When first cast down, chained to the flesh	167
When I am away	331
When I first saw your lady kneel	242
When I was a boy I searched the skies	138
When the first sweet burst of love and lust	107
When you pulled at the wheel with me	317
When you were first deceived beyond your trust	248
'Where are you going,' I heard her say	404
Where have you gone to, Mary Boots	75
Where once the Spring	406

Who can say when all this was begun	
Why don't you visit me	137
Why do you tear at	213
Why is it always a summer's day	71
Wild horses we	220
Wild winter bird, your same old graces	90
'Will someone buy this year of mine?	89
With all the art of patient mending	225
With what enchanted breath has woman	200
Woman, Oh Woman	407
Words roll free from a tongue sometime	108
Would Cook, I wonder, ever have dreamt	38
You are God's best kept secret, Yao Li rong	371
You ask me, where would I wish to lie	65
You brought your Bibles and printed tracts	365
You built your stone cottages	197
You lie a-doze beneath a buttercup	313
You may believe, my ladies dear	391
You never knew I loved	274
Your eyes bright, eager and trusting	322
Your way, at last, has gone from me	166
You stand with all your comrades in the van	359
You think that I	290
You think that you only	326
'You think you can walk away from this	172
You, who sit beneath your tree of birds	270
You with all your art	421
You've gone again, and I sit granite faced	314

www.ingramcontent.com/pod-product-compliance
Lightning Source LLC
Chambersburg PA
CBHW050118170426
43197CB00011B/1630